Toddler Brain Basics

twelve to 24 months

Everything you need to know to nurture your toddler's developing mind

Brilliant!
Beginnings™

Brilliant! Beginnings™

Brilliant Beginnings, LLC
P.O. Box 13050
Long Beach, CA 90803

www.brilliantbeginnings.com
Tel: (800) 432-1357

Made in the USA.

First Edition.

Library of Congress Catalog Card Number: 99-90992
ISBN 1-929651-00-7

Table of Contents

"Early experiences are so powerful...they can completely change the way a person turns out."
HARRY CHUGANI, PEDIATRIC NEUROBIOLOGIST

In the second year of your toddler's life, you can almost see and hear her brain at work. She spends 20 minutes turning a shape sorter around in her hands trying to make sense of its color and function; she points to and names every object in her bedroom, trying out the strange and wonderful sounds of language; and she confidently assumes the posture of independence, only to cast it off as being too much too soon – for the moment, anyway. It may seem as if the biggest job you have is to try to keep up with all the amazing changes, but you have a far more important role than that: you have the opportunity to shape your toddler's brain and influence her ability to learn throughout her lifetime.

This opportunity has only recently been recognized. In the past, we could only guess about the way in which the delicate dance between nature (genes) and nurture (experiences) produces a unique human being with a unique brain; it was generally thought that genetics influenced a person's development far more than the environment. Recent technological advances in science, such as Positron Emission Tomography (PET) and Magnetic Resolution Imaging (MRI) scans, have given us evidence of the way a child's brain is organized and how it grows. We now know that your toddler's brain uses experiences as nourishment to shape itself, and that the more experiences it has, the better shape it will be in to learn. This is true whether she's learning that a cat says "meow," or learning how to build a bridge, a government or a network of powerful PCs.

What this means for you as a parent of a 12- to 24-month-old is that you can influence how your toddler's brain develops through the experiences you provide for her. Holding your toddler in your lap while you sing and act out "The Itsy Bitsy Spider," for example, strengthens certain pathways in the brain, and influences how all the brain's cells will work together for the rest of your toddler's life.

Nobody knows exactly which pathways will be influenced, but the research strongly shows that the overall result of an enriched environment is a more efficient neural network. So is singing a song once enough? What about singing it twice? What exactly does it take to create an enriched environment? This Guidebook will help you find out.

You may have learned a few tips from having other children, talking to other mothers, or reading publications devoted to other topics, but you owe it to your toddler to possess a more comprehensive understanding of how to nurture her developing brain.

Brilliant Beginnings is committed to giving you the knowledge and know-how you need. We have brought together a board of advisors, whose specializations cover a broad range of scientific and parenting disciplines, including the neurosciences, child development, early childhood music, language development, early education and parenting practices. With this team of experts (whose biographies appear on page 5), we are developing a full line of consumer products that provide clear, concise and constructive information on early intellectual development. The goal of all of our products, is to help you put this information into action.

Toddler Brain Basics Guidebook: 12- to 24-Months

Throughout *Toddler Brain Basics Guidebook: 12- to 24-Months* we use "he" and "she" in alternating sections, so at least we'll get your toddler's gender right half the time!

The Information Sections

Toddler Brain Basics Guidebook: 12- to 24- Months begins with seven sections devoted to understanding your toddler's developing mind – not only how it continues to grow, but also what it needs to be its best:

1. **Your Toddler's Developing Brain:** Provides a critical foundation for understanding how experiences lead to physical changes in the brain which in turn help your toddler progress from a walking, talking one-year-old to an opinionated, problem-solving two-year-old.

2. **Learning in the Toddler Years:** Explains how your toddler's brain is primed to learn certain concepts, such as the permanence of objects, cause-and-effect relationships and how things fit into categories, and shows you how experiences reinforce those lessons.

3. **Growing Language Skills:** Toddlers from 12 to 24 months experience a huge boost in language production and comprehension. Experiences that expose them to a wide

range of words and sounds take advantage of this natural propensity to learn.

4. **Pre-Literacy:** Explains how reading is a skill that develops gradually over time and shows you how to gently introduce your toddler to the sound and story skills needed for future literacy.

5. **Social and Emotional Development:** Describes the link between intellectual and emotional development, and how changes in the brain enable your toddler to see herself as a separate individual and seek independence from mom and dad.

6. **Music's Impact on Development:** Explains how early exposure and training in music has a long-lasting and profound effect on your toddler's musical and intellectual development.

7. **Monitoring Your Toddler's Development:** Checkpoints designed to give you an objective view of your toddler's development.

The Action Sections: Ages and Stages

The second half of our Parent Guidebook is devoted to putting your newfound knowledge to work. We help you create a nurturing and enriching environment in which your toddler can flourish – both now and throughout his lifetime. To this end, we provide you with ideas, activities, inspiration and advice so you can nurture both your toddler's intellectual development and the trusting relationship that will enable him to become an independent person; we give you the know-how to make intellectual development part of your natural daily routine.

Parents are a young child's most influential teachers; what you teach will profoundly influence your child's entire life. This can seem like a daunting responsibility, but it's also an unbelievable opportunity. Our goal is to help you take advantage of this opportunity every day. Providing your toddler with an enriched, stimulating environment can be as simple as playing hide-and-seek, climbing up to the big slide at the park or snuggling up to read a favorite book.

The Resource Section

At the back of the *Toddler Brain Basics Guidebook™*, you will find a **Resources Section** that points you to additional sources of information (websites, organizations, articles and books) covering a wide range of topics related to parenting, child development and nurturing your child's developing mind.

Website

Visit our website at **www.brilliantbeginnings.com** to learn more about our full line of products, to receive updates on the latest findings in brain research and child development, to search our book review and resource databases and to share ideas with our community of experts, parents and caregivers who are just as passionate about nurturing your toddler's intellectual development as you are.

Our Commitment

At **Brilliant Beginnings**, we believe that children have an unlimited potential for learning and that parents have an unequalled opportunity to help them realize that potential by exposing them to an enriched environment during the critical early years of life. Our mission is to:

- Provide the information you need to nurture your toddler's developing mind.

- Keep you up-to-date on the latest scientific research about learning, the brain and overall intellectual development.

- Explain what the research means and how to incorporate it into your child's everyday life through fun, enriching activities.

- Help you understand the process of how your child learns at various ages and stages, so you are better equipped to nurture your child's potential and identify areas where your child might need extra support.

- Direct you to additional information through expert-recommended websites, books, articles and organizations.

Advisory Board

The experts on our advisory board play an integral role in the development of **Brilliant Beginnings** parent kits. They actively participate throughout the entire development process from brainstorming to recommending what research to present to reviewing final drafts of sections. We are proud to have each one of these specialists on our team, and are grateful for their input:

- **Stevanne Auerbach, Ph.D., Children's Products Expert**
  Dr. Stevanne Auerbach, also known as Dr. Toy, is an expert in play, toys, children's products, early education, parent education, child development and special education. Dr. Auerbach produces *Dr. Toy's Guide*: the first online magazine to report on toys and children's products. The site contains reports based on her annual awards presented in *Dr. Toy's 100 Best Children's Products*, in which she selects and evaluates the newest and best toys. It includes other products and features like *Best Classic Toys* and *Best Vacation Products*. Dr. Auerbach is the Director of the Institute for Childhood Resources. She is the author of *Dr. Toy's Smart Play: How to Raise a Child with a High P.Q. (Play Quotient)* and she serves as a consultant and speaker on play.

- **Angela Ballantyne, Ph.D., Pediatric Neuropsychologist**

  Dr. Ballantyne is an expert in the area of Clinical Psychology, with an emphasis in assessment of young children. She is an Assistant Project Neuroscientist at the University of California, San Diego, School of Medicine, having oversight responsibility for many of the developmental evaluation studies being conducted at the university. Dr. Ballantyne has numerous publications in the area of cognitive assessment, and has served as reviewer for a number of texts on the subject.

- **Les Cohen, Ph.D., Professor of Developmental Psychology**

  Dr. Cohen is Professor of Developmental Psychology, and Director of the Children's Research Laboratory at the University of Texas at Austin. He is also the founding editor of the journal, *Infancy*, which covers a broad range of issues specific to early development. Dr. Cohen is a renowned expert in the field of early cognitive development, with a primary focus on the influence of environmental factors in the development of memory and cognition of infants. Dr. Cohen's research centers on how infants process and use visual and auditory information in their environment.

- **Lori Davidson, M.S., Director of Early Childhood Education**

  Ms. Davidson has served as the Director of Early Childhood Education Programs at the Long Beach, California, Jewish Community Center for the past 15 years. Ms. Davidson manages a center, serving over 200 children, ranging in age from six months to five years, is an expert in developmentally appropriate practices for children spanning this entire age range.

- **Tish Davison, Children's Playthings Expert**

  Tish Davidson is an expert in the developmental appropriateness of children's playthings, and serves as an independent toy and game reviewer and consultant. She also authors a syndicated column on child development and family issues and has contributed to textbooks on early childhood education and pediatric health.

- **Kathy Hirsh-Pasek, Ph.D., Professor of Developmental Psychology**

  Dr. Hirsh-Pasek is Professor of Psychology at Temple University, specializing in early cognitive development, language growth and applied cognition in preschool and early elementary aged children. She is the co-author of three books: *Academic Instruction in Early Childhood: Challenge or Pressure; The Origins Of Grammar: Evidence From Comprehension;* and *How Babies Talk: The Magic and Mystery of Language Acquisition in The First Three Years*. She has authored numerous articles on early childhood development, with topics ranging from language growth, reading development and early academic achievement. She is also on the editorial board of the journal *Infancy*.

- **Lynn Kleiner, Early Childhood Music Expert**

  Lynn Kleiner is founder and director of *Music Rhapsody*, a music school for parents, infants, toddlers and children up through age 13. Ms. Kleiner has pioneered an 'active' approach to music programs, with families learning music while actively participating in the music through dance, movement, the playing of instruments and singing. Ms. Kleiner has presented at numerous Orff Schulwerk Association and National Music Educators conferences, as well as state conferences for music education in the United States and Australia. She has also given workshops for preschools, school districts, Orff Chapters and parent groups, nationwide.

- **Debra Mills, Ph.D., Cognitive Developmental Neuroscientist**
Dr. Mills is the Director of the Brain and Cognitive Development Laboratory, and an Assistant Research Scientist at the Center for Research in Language at the University of California, San Diego. Dr. Mills' research focuses on developmental changes in brain organization for language and non-language cognitive functions. She sits on the editorial board of the *Journal of Developmental Neuropsychology*, and has been a reviewer for the National Institute of Health, *Child Development*, *Neuropsychologia*, *Developmental Psychology* and *Developmental Neuropsychology*.

- **Claire B Kopp, Applied Developmental Psychologist**
Dr. Kopp is a professor of applied developmental psychology at the Claremont Graduate University, a Fellow of the American Psychological Association and past editor of the *Newsletter of the Society for Research in Child Development*. Dr. Kopp's research focuses on early social and emotional development, including self regulation in young children and factors that contribute to developmental risk. She has published extensively and is currently co-editor of the *Guilford Series on Social and Emotional Development*, and is also the author of *Baby Steps: The 'Why's' of Your Child's Behavior in the First Two Years*.

- **Nora Newcombe, Ph.D., Professor of Developmental Psychology**
Dr. Newcombe is currently a professor and Head of the Cognitive Division in the Department of Psychology at Temple University. She was formerly on the faculty of Pennsylvania State University, has twice been a Visiting Professor at the University of Pennsylvania and will visit Princeton University in 1999-2000 supported by a Cattell Fellowship. Her research interests are in spatial development and memories of early childhood experiences. She is editor of the *Journal of Experimental Psychology: General*, former Associate Editor of *Psychological Bulletin*, and was the Program Co-Chair for the 1997 Society for Research in Child Development meetings.

- **Cecilia Riddell, Ph.D., Professor of Early Childhood Music**
Dr. Riddell teaches infant and toddler music classes at the Pasadena Conservatory of Music, and has taught music and music education at California State University at Dominguez Hills, and California State University at Northridge. Dr. Riddell is a member of the Music Educators National Conference, and has authored numerous articles and workshops on early childhood music for local, state, national and international music associations. She was named "Teacher of the Year" in 1994 by the California Music Educators Association, Southern Section; and along with Lynn Kleiner, recently co-authored a book for parents and teachers, *"Kids Make Music; Toddlers Make Music Too!"*

Acknowledgements

Brilliant Beginnings would like to thank everyone involved in developing *Toddler Brain Basics* especially our Parent Panel. Their time, insights and experience have enabled us to make sure that the information and ideas we bring to you are meaningful, accurate, appropriate and useful.

The Brilliant Beginnings Editorial Team

EDITOR-IN-CHIEF:
Kathleen Healy

MANAGING EDITOR/LEAD RESEARCHER:
Jaime Goldfarb, Ph.D.

ART DIRECTOR:
Corinne Zeutzius

WRITER:
Jennie Nash

RESEARCHERS:
Benjamin Eller
Marisa Fernandez
Kimberly Johnson
John Lubbers
Susan Neufeld
Melissa Schweisguth

COPY EDITORS:
Debora Smith

The Brilliant Beginnings Parent Review Panel

The following parents made recommendations on what to include in the guidebook, read working drafts, reviewed final drafts and shared their personal experiences of parenting:

Suzette Abend

Terri Alenikov

Veronica Barnes

Stacey Cochrane

Jay Cywan

Miriam Cywan

Michael Franco

Michelle Franco

Beth Holden

Jeff Housman

Maureen Housman

Ellen Ivanov

Christine Knight

Susan Laker

Sue Law

Liz MacDonald

Susan Middlesworth

Grace Mori

Barbara McGuire

Lisa Ann Olsen

Joy Pagaza

Paola Pennington

Jennie Robertson

Allanah Rosenberg

Karen Schiele

Renita Smith

Nancy Stressling

Mary Tenberge

Jacqui Viale

Karla von Schroter

Leslie Wells

Sandy Witz

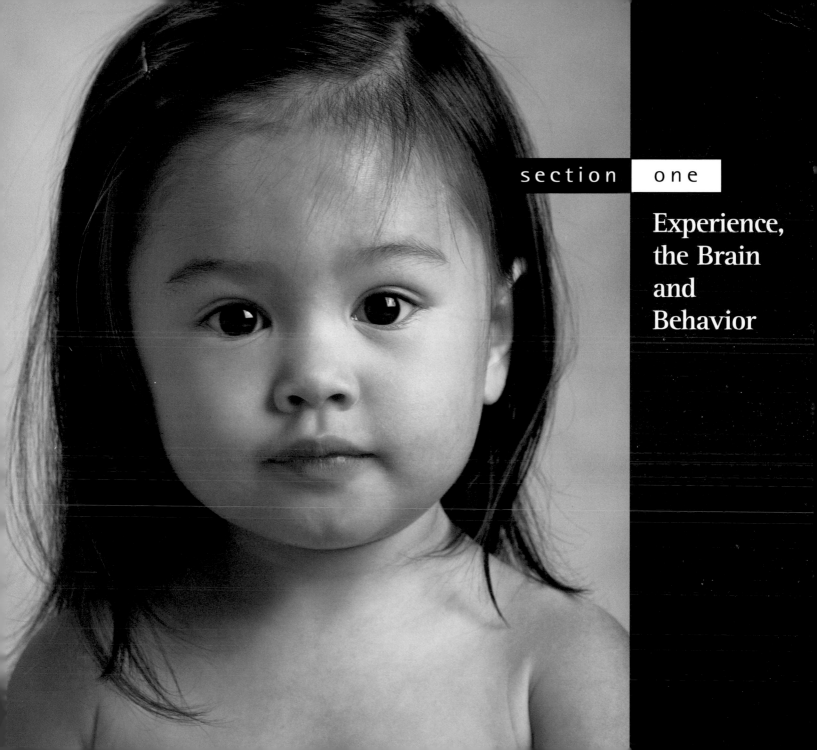

section one

Experience,
the Brain
and
Behavior

Experience, the Brain and Behavior

What You'll Discover In This Section

"The empires of the future are the empires of the mind."

WINSTON CHURCHILL, STATESMAN

- How early experiences enhance the brain's wiring.

- How changes in the structure of your toddler's brain affect behavior.

- Why specific types of experiences are crucial during "windows of opportunity."

- How changes in the brain and advances in language are related.

"The brain is wider than the sky."

EMILY DICKINSON, POET

Your toddler has been given many gifts – his mommy's smile, his daddy's eyes, his grandmother's calm disposition. He's also been given a genetic blueprint that sets the basic foundation for his intellectual, physical and emotional development. These blueprints, however, are just that – the basic design for development. In order to maximize the potential of these plans, toddlers require input from their environment; and what your toddler needs most is an environment that provides ongoing, rich, varied and stimulating experiences.

Research conducted in the past decade tells us that a child's environment plays a vital role in the formation of the structure of his brain. The brain starts out as a flexible organ whose various regions process a wide range of different information. In the adult brain, for example, language is specialized in the left hemisphere; a toddler's brain, however, has not yet reached that level of specialization and has the tendency to process language in both hemispheres. The experiences of the first few years of life are what alter the brain's structure; through experience, your toddler's brain gradually develops into a highly organized adult brain that devotes distinct areas to specialized tasks.

The neural structures created as a result of early experiences have a huge impact on your toddler's intellectual abilities. The more early opportunities he has to learn, the more information he can take in throughout his lifetime. The good news for parents is that these early opportunities don't have to be anything heroic. They are common, enjoyable everyday experiences such as conversation, observation, song, dance and play. These things may seem small, mundane or even downright repetitious, but it is clear that, over time, they make the difference in the future function of your toddler's brain.

The Miracle of a Toddler's Brain

Why do our brains require all this additional attention? Why are humans born with incomplete brain wiring? It seems like a very inefficient setup, since it makes human babies dependent for such a prolonged period of time. The incompleteness, however, is exactly what enables humans to adapt to almost any environment into which we are born. A newborn horse may be up and running with the herd within days of its birth, but a horse won't ever learn how to speak, to read, to write or to conduct the Los Angeles Philharmonic. Since humans require input from the world around us to complete our neural circuitry, we can create a neural circuitry that can most efficiently deal with our environment. We can create a neural circuitry that is designed to learn and keep learning. It turns out to be a rather miraculous setup.

"Early experiences organize a baby's brain for a lifetime of learning."

DEBRA MILLS, COGNITIVE DEVELOPMENTAL NEUROSCIENTIST

Supporting Evidence

Elizabeth Bates and her colleagues at the University of California at San Diego tracked the language acquisition of 53 children who suffered serious brain trauma in one hemisphere of their brain prior to six months of age. The researchers wanted to know whether damage to the left hemisphere precluded a child from developing language skills, since for 95 percent of normal adults, the left hemisphere is where language is processed. The study found that the children who suffered brain damage were not able to develop language skills in the same way that non-injured children do, but they were able to communicate quite effectively. They demonstrated some early delays in their acquisition of language (those with injuries in their right hemisphere were at greater risk to experience delays in word comprehension and gesture; those with injuries to their left hemisphere experienced more delays in the onset of their expressive vocabulary) but these children, on average, fell well within the normal range on tests measuring word comprehension, word production and gesturing. It appears that the infant brain is plastic enough to form alternative pathways for language acquisition that enable them to communicate quite effectively.

KEY-POINT
"Early experiences help sculpt a toddler's brain."

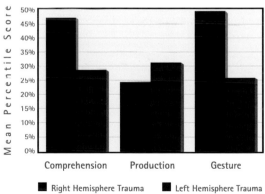

Toddler's with Early Brain Trauma Can Still Develop Language Skills in the Normal Range

Mean Percentile Score

Comprehension   Production   Gesture

■ Right Hemisphere Trauma   ■ Left Hemisphere Trauma

Bates, E., Thal, D., Trauner, D., Fenson, J., Aram, D., Eisele, J., and Nass, R. (1997). From First Words to Grammar in Children With Focal Brain Injury. *Developmental Neuropsychology*, 13(3), 275-343.

An Efficient Brain Leads to Efficient Learning

Information is transmitted through the brain via neurons, or nerve cells, which form a complex network of circuits. The learning capacity of the brain is determined by the richness of memories stored in the network and how easily information flows across this network:

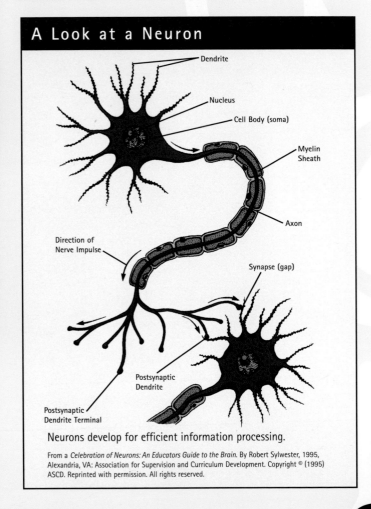

A Look at a Neuron

Dendrite

Nucleus

Cell Body (soma)

Myelin Sheath

Axon

Direction of Nerve Impulse

Synapse (gap)

Postsynaptic Dendrite

Postsynaptic Dendrite Terminal

Neurons develop for efficient information processing.

- As information is transmitted from your toddler's eyes, ears, nose, mouth and skin, an electrical impulse is generated.

- This impulse is transmitted from neuron to neuron via chemicals known as neurotransmitters.

- Neurons never actually touch each other. There is a small gap, or synapse, between them where the neurotransmitters flow. Through this flow of chemicals, messages are passed along from one neuron to the next.

- Scientists believe that much of what we call learning takes place in this transmission of information across the neurons. A neuron may emit a neurotransmitter that tells one nearby neuron to fire (meaning pass on the impulse) and another nearby neuron not to fire.

- The entire pattern that emerges results in information flowing along unique and specific pathways, with unique and specific associations and memories being created along the way. Those associations and memories add up to learning.

ACTIVITY
Take an old hat – one that is deep enough to hide objects dropped into it, but shallow enough for your toddler to reach the bottomt – and take turns dropping in blocks. You can count them as they go in, name their color or drop them in a special order.

BENEFIT
Exercises fine motor skills, strengthens memory skills and teaches numbers and language concepts.

Early Experiences Shape the Brain

It can be difficult to grasp the concept that early experiences shape the brain; it's a relatively new concept, it's a really big concept, and it's not a concept that's being talked about at the corner coffee house. There is a great deal of evidence, however, which supports the case. This evidence comes from studies on everything from synaptic density, to the cells that support the brain, to the fatty sheath that insulates the neurons, to the way that blood flows through the brain. While you may not be in the habit of reading neuroscience journals, it's exciting to understand exactly what early experiences are doing to all these aspects of the brain, and to know exactly how much these experiences matter.

Experiences Build and Prune Synaptic Connections

One of the most amazing facts about the brain is that by the age of three, your child will have an estimated 1,000 trillion synaptic connections – approximately twice as many connections as you do. Throughout the course of childhood, this number will be pared down so that by about age 15, the number of your child's synaptic connections will be closer to yours. The pruning down process of the synaptic connections is governed by early experiences. The pruning process is important because having an overabundance of synaptic connections slows the flow of information in the brain. It is as if the chemicals don't know which of the many available paths to take. What experiences do, in effect, is create superhighways in the neural networks of the brain-well-worn paths that are better able to process information. The synapses that are not well used wither and die in a process that scientists refer to as "synaptogenesis." That is why the more, and the richer, experiences a toddler has, the more efficient the neural network that results.

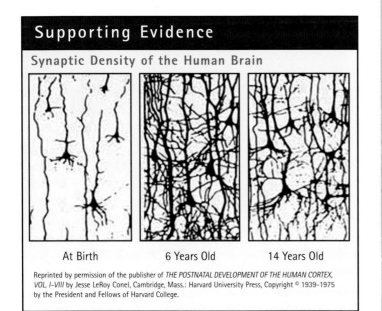

Supporting Evidence

Synaptic Density of the Human Brain

| At Birth | 6 Years Old | 14 Years Old |

Reprinted by permission of the publisher of *THE POSTNATAL DEVELOPMENT OF THE HUMAN CORTEX, VOL. I-VIII* by Jesse LeRoy Conel, Cambridge, Mass.: Harvard University Press, Copyright © 1939-1975 by the President and Fellows of Harvard College.

What's a Parent To Do?

ACTIVITY

As a part of your bathtime ritual, wrap some of your child's favorite bath toys in washcloths. Line them up beside the bath, or sink, and let him discover what's inside. Throw in the occasional surprise, such as his shampoo bottle or a tube of toothpaste.

BENEFIT

A ritual that develops memory skills and encourages social skills.

Experiences Impact the Supporting Structures of the Brain

In addition to neurons and synapses, the brain also contains a large number of supporting cells, called glial cells. Until recently, scientists didn't believe glial cells did much more than hold the brain together. New findings, however, indicate that these cells play a vital role in information processing. Glial cells:

- Provide physical support for the neurons.

- Guide the direction of the growth of axons – the long central body of a neuron.

- Insulate neurons for greater efficiency.

- Modulate activity within the synapses.

- Regulate how dense the synaptic connections become.

- Influence the release of neurotransmitters.

- Influence the flow of blood to the brain.

Neuroscientists have recently found that both the size and number of glial cells can be affected by environmental conditions, which is yet another reason why it's so beneficial to play all those games and sing all those songs to your toddler. The findings indicate that animals reared in complex, challenging and interesting environments produce

Supporting Evidence

Synaptic Connections Are Pruned Through Experience

How do we know that the number of synaptic connections in the brain follows a first up and then down growth pattern? Neuroscientist Peter Huttenlocher at the University of Chicago has painstakingly counted the number of connections in the brain at key points in development. The results confirm that at birth, infants are born with approximately 50 trillion synaptic connections, which is the same number of synaptic connections as an adult.

KEY-POINT
"Experiences prune the connections in a toddler's brain to make it more efficient."

By age three, the number of connections has approximately doubled. Through experience, the number of connections is reduced so that by the time your child is 15 years old, the total number of connections will be at approximately the same level as that of an adult.

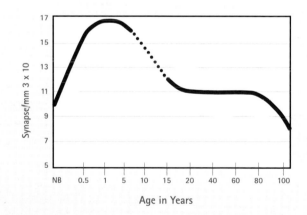

Early Experiences Build Neural Pathways
the Most Used Pathways will Remain

Reproduced with permission of Elsevier/North-Holland Biomedical press. From Huttenlocher, P.R. (1979). Synaptic Density in Human Frontal Cortex—Developmental Changes and Effects of Aging. *Brain Research, 163*, 195-205.

more, and larger, glial cells than animals reared in less stimulating environments. The result is thought to be an improvement in the ability of the brain to transfer information. It is important to note that these benefits do not occur overnight. Glial cell changes result only after a long period of exposure to an enriched environment – as long, in some cases, as a month. The lesson for parents, of course, is to feel confident that the enriched environment you are providing will benefit your child for many years to come.

Changes at the Cellular Level

Not only do early experiences shape the synaptic pathways in the brain and boost the number of glial cells, they also increase the number of neurons that become myelinated – a key cellular development. Myelin is a fatty coating that surrounds some of the neurons in the brain and performs a number of critical functions related to information processing. Myelin:

- Helps electrical impulses travel more quickly across the neurons, which results in the brain being able to process more information, at a faster rate.

- Helps each neuron fire in rapid succession – after a neuron transmits an impulse, there is a time period in which it is unable to fire again. Myelin reduces this time period, enabling the brain to pass more information in a shorter period of time.

- Leads the neuron to commit to processing only certain types of information, which makes the brain more efficient, and less flexible.

It used to be believed that myelination of neurons was governed solely by genetic influences. New evidence from studies conducted with rats (who make a good proxy for studying the inner workings of the human brain since their neuroanatomy parallels our own) indicates that being raised in an enriched environment can increase the number of neurons that become myelinated.

Blood Flow Increases

The changes that occur in the brain in response to enriched environments – the creation of a more complex and efficient neural network, increased myelination and increased number of glial cells – demand increased blood flow in the brain. Researchers have found that as the level of complexity in the environment goes up, so does the number of new "micro-capillaries" that are formed in the brain; impoverished environments produce far fewer capillaries than enriched ones. Increased blood flow is one of the reasons why a brain that is stimulated in the early years turns into a brain that functions at a higher level in future years. Not only is the cellular groundwork laid for learning, but the means to keep those cells nourished is laid, as well.

Supporting Evidence

Synaptic Connections and the Environment

William T. Greenough worked with his colleagues, James E. Black and Anita M. Sirevaag at the University of Illinois, Urbana-Champaign to look at how processes in the brain are altered by environmental factors. As with their study on glial cells, the researchers looked at three groups of rats – one group raised in a stimulating complex environment, one in a social pair environment and one in isolation. The researchers found that there were increases in synaptic connections, just as there were increases in glial cells. What they also found was that there was an increase in the number of capillaries providing vital blood flow to the connections, but this increase was only significant in young rats. The formation of new capillaries was substantially impaired in middle-aged animals and almost absent for old rats.

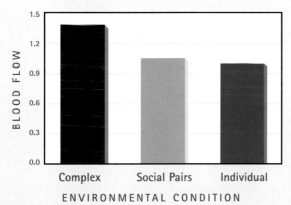

Complex Environments Create Greater Blood Flow in the Brain

Reproduced with permission of Elsevier/North-Holland Biomedical press. From Black, J.E., Sirevaag, A.M., Greenough, W.T., (1987). Complex experience promotes capillary formation in young rat visual cortex, *Neuroscience Letters, 83*, 351-355.

"It is believed by many that the biological 'window of opportunity' when learning is efficient and easily retained is perhaps not fully exploited by our educational system."

HARRY CHUGANI, PEDIATRIC NEUROBIOLOGIST

Taking Advantage of Windows of Opportunity

The term "Windows of Opportunity" has been a recent favorite in the popular press. The implication seems to be that there are some exact periods during which learning must take place or forever be lost. As a result, there has been some pressure to identify and define these exact windows and design some type of curriculum around them. Science, however, has yet to provide any such neat and tidy map.

What we do have is evidence of general timeframes during which learning happens more easily and efficiently than it does at later points in time. For example:

- The visual and auditory systems need environmental input during the first few months in order to form "normal" neural connections in the brain. If deprived of this input, the neural connections may never form correctly, and will therefore inhibit a child's ability to process sights and sounds normally.

The Sensitive Period for Vision

In one of the seminal pieces of work in the area of Sensitive Periods, David H. Hubel and Torsten N. Wiesel, of Harvard University, were interested in why children born with congenital cataracts in one eye often continued to suffer blindness in that eye, even after the cataracts had been removed. To replicate this in an experimental condition, they sewed shut one of the eyelids of newborn kittens, as well as one eyelid of older cats. Of foremost concern was the impact that loss of visual input would have on cats of differing ages. The findings were clear: young kittens remained blind in the eye sewn shut even after the eye was opened. This blindness resulted because the neurons responsible for sight in that eye did not form connections with other neurons. Furthermore, the neurons in the bad eye created connections to help the good eye process information. This finding did not hold for adult cats, who regained their normal vision once the eye was opened. The results indicate that there is a specific period early in the life when neurons need the appropriate environmental conditions to create appropriate connections in the brain and, if deprived of this experience, the result can yield long-term, if not permanent effects in the brain. As a result of this work, doctors now routinely remove congenital cataracts in people prior to this critical window, usually before a child is two months old.

"Iron rusts from disuse, stagnant water loses its purity and in cold weather becomes frozen; even so does inaction sap the vigors of the mind."

LEONARDO DA VINCI

PHILOSOPHER, PAINTER, SCULPTOR, MATHEMATICIAN

- Children must hear the sounds of language at critical periods during the first few years of life in order to be able to process, and even identify, the specific sounds of a language. If deprived of these sounds, they can eventually learn language, but the task becomes significantly harder. For this reason, the regular hearing tests your pediatrician does as part of the well-baby check are important for toddlers; if a toddler is not hearing well, it will be hard for him to produce the sounds of language well, and hard to acquire the skills needed to read.

The best way to take advantage of the windows of learning opportunity is to expose your child to an environment filled with words, sounds, pictures, textures, books, music, objects and opportunities to play and explore. In this way, you will naturally nurture the brain at every stage of development in every area of learning, and you will prepare your child for countless learning opportunities in the future. There's no need to rush out to buy any learning aids, fancy toys, or to enroll your child in special classes. You are probably already doing exactly the kind of activities your toddler needs; all most parents need is what we're here to provide: a little more insight, a lot of inspiration and concrete ideas for continuing down the path toward enrichment.

What's a Parent To Do?

ACTIVITY

Create a daily walk ritual. Go at approximately the same time each day and go on the same route. Point out landmarks as you go and look for things that have changed – such as trees, gardens, the color of someone's house, etc.

BENEFIT

A comforting social ritual that exercises memory skills and muscle coordination.

The Brain and Behavior

I t seems obvious that your toddler's brain is controlling his behavior. What is not so obvious to the casual observer is that changes in a toddler's brain lead to more complex behaviors. It can be hard, in other words, to believe that all this nurturing works. What's exciting for parents is that we have concrete evidence that it does. Starting in the first year, and continuing throughout childhood, there are examples of how changes in the structure of the brain are related to changes in behavior. Early experiences create a more efficient brain, which, in turn, enables your toddler to use the word "juice" when

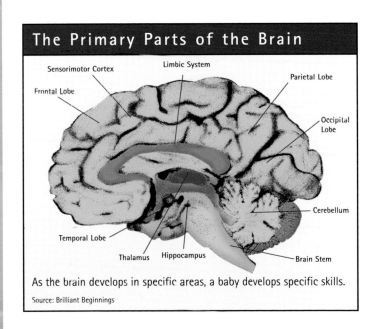

The Primary Parts of the Brain

Sensorimotor Cortex
Limbic System
Parietal Lobe
Frontal Lobe
Occipital Lobe
Temporal Lobe
Thalamus
Hippocampus
Cerebellum
Brain Stem

As the brain develops in specific areas, a baby develops specific skills.

Source: Brilliant Beginnings

he wants a drink and to stop himself from throwing a toy when he can't get it to work. We outline three of the most dramatic examples, below:

Energy Usage

Harry Chugani, pediatric neurobiologist at Wayne State University, has found that a baby's brain devotes more energy to the areas responsible for the greatest growth. It's difficult to tell whether the changes in usage stem from changes in activity, or vice versa, but it is clear that the behavior you see in a baby is related to the activity in his brain:

- Prior to three months, much of your baby's behavior is based on reflexes. At this time, the majority of energy is used by subcortical areas, such as the brain stem – the area responsible for controlling reflexes.

- After the third month, your baby begins to reach for everything in sight. At this time, energy activity is increasing around the thalamus – the area responsible for reaching movements.

- Around eight months, your child is beginning to demonstrate higher level intellectual functioning (such as a knowledge of the permanence of objects). At this time, energy activity is increasing in the prefrontal cortex – the area responsible for higher level processes.

What's a Parent To Do?

ACTIVITY

Add a few drops of food coloring to a few dollops of whipped cream. Let your toddler paint – and eat – his sweet finger paints.

BENEFIT

An edible lesson in colors and shapes that develops fine motor skills.

Language

One of the clearest examples of the relationship between brain development and behavior is demonstrated with language. In adults, the processing of language takes place primarily in the left hemisphere. This is not the whole story, however, with young children. While toddlers do tend to process language in the left hemisphere, the right hemisphere is also involved; the complete specialization of brain structures does not occur until much later, perhaps not even until early adulthood. As your toddler reaches various language milestones, there is a dramatic change in the organization of language-relevant brain systems; with each jump in language ability, the brain becomes more specialized for processing language.

Response Inhibition

Developmental psychologists now believe that one of the major advances a toddler makes during the second year of life is his ability to stop himself from doing things. Take the example of separation anxiety. Many children develop this anxiety around the end of the first year, and then seem to get over it later in the second year.

Researchers believe that this transition is related to a toddler's developing ability to inhibit an initial response – in this case, reacting with fear – as a parent leaves. It has been shown that these types of emotional reactions are generated in the right hemisphere of the brain. In order for a toddler not to act upon this immediate impulse, an inhibitory signal has to be received from the left hemisphere. The timing of a child's ability to inhibit behaviors coincides almost perfectly with the development of fibers in the corpus callosum – the part of the brain that enables the right and left hemispheres to communicate. Scientists now believe that this development enables the inhibitory signals to be sent and received, so that a toddler can now stop himself from acting on impulse.

What's a Parent To Do?

ACTIVITY

If you or your spouse will be away for an evening, record yourself reading one of your toddler's favorite books. At storytime, instruct whoever's home to play the recording.

BENEFIT

A comforting ritual that reinforces a love of reading.

Supporting Evidence

How the Brain Becomes Specialized for Processing Language

Dr. Debra Mills, Developmental Cognitive Neuroscientist at the University of California, San Diego, has been conducting groundbreaking research on the relationship between changes in structures in the brain and the development of language skills. In one recent study, Dr. Mills looked at the brain wave patterns of infants ranging from 13 to 20 months old. The infants watched a moving puppet "speak" words that the infants either knew or words that they did not yet comprehend (based on parental reports). The results indicated that in infants 13-17 months old, words they understood elicited more brain activity, over both the left and right sides of the brain, than words they did not yet understand. In comparison, by 20-months of age these differences in brain activity were more specialized and apparent in only the temporal and parietal regions on the left side of the brain. The change in brain organization was linked to the dramatic increases in vocabulary size that toddlers experience at this time.

Learning
in the
Toddler
Years

Learning in the Toddler Years

"*Learning is not attained by chance, it must be sought for with ardor and attended to with diligence.*"

ABIGAIL ADAMS, WIFE OF JOHN ADAMS, THE SECOND PRESIDENT OF THE UNITED STATES

What You'll Discover | In This Section

- How play and learning go hand-in-hand.

- How your toddler's ability to remember events and emotions grows.

- How a better sense of space and time helps toddlers navigate the world.

- How your toddler learns about the intentions of other people, and how this enables her to operate efficiently in her environment.

23

"By providing children with challenging experiences through enriched education and environments, those dendrites cannot help but be off to a good start!"
MARIAN CLEAVES DIAMOND, NEUROBIOLOGIST

Learning is Child's Play

For the relative who visits your house every few weeks, it may seem as if your toddler is developing by leaps and bounds. Every time the relative shows up, your toddler has a new skill or a new word to show off. But what the part-time observer doesn't see are all the small steps – such as two-sound babbling or crawling backward down the stairs – that lead up to those seemingly mind-boggling advances.

Every major advance your child enjoys during the second year is proceeded by months of small observations and experiences. She's eager to explore her world because she now knows, from months of finding puzzle pieces behind the couch, that things exist even when she can't see them. She loves games of cause-and-effect, such as pop-up toys, because she has been learning, from the first days of her

life, that one action can cause another. She is insistent on climbing into her own car seat because she finally understands that she is separate from you and capable of taking care of herself in certain key ways. For the toddler, small incremental changes in knowledge lead to huge changes in behavior.

The way a toddler gains all this knowledge is through play, be it structured or spontaneous, shared with a parent or solitary. Play is the single most powerful learning tool she has. Through play, she learns about object permanence, cause-and-effect relationships, space-time relationships and the abilities and limitations of her own body and mind. The richer a toddler's play, the richer her understanding of the world – not only throughout the early years but for the rest of her life.

Key Milestones in Learning

Age	Milestone
12 to 15 Months	• Increased Locomotion — a higher level of gross motor skills becomes evident. • Increased Coordination of Objects — at 12 months, she begins to coordinate two objects in her play, *e.g.*, she picks up two blocks so she can bang them together. • Increased Imitation — she uses an object in the same functional way as an adult would use it, *e.g.*, bangs hammers or puts a spoon in her mouth.
15 to 18 Months	• Increased Imagination — she uses objects playfully, *e.g.*, waves a spoon around in the air for fun. • Body Awareness — she now is aware of, and can identify, many parts of her own and other people's bodies.
18 to 21 Months	• Recall of Specific Events and Specific Emotions — her ability to recall the details of specific events, and how she felt during those events, increases. • Imagination Leads to Abstraction — instead of pretending that she is going to sleep, she now pretends her bear is going to sleep. • Selfhood — she begins to develop a sense of identity, selfhood.
21 to 24 Months	• Self Regulation — she is now better able to stop herself from doing things she would previously have done on impulse. • Understanding the Intentions of Others — she now has a growing sense of when someone does something on purpose or by accident. • Cooperation with Others — her play begins to involve more interaction and involvement with others. • Understanding of Symbols — she treats objects as if they were something else, *e.g.*, drinks water but calls it tea, bakes a cake using sand. • Imagination Takes Off — the meanings of objects and actions are transformed to fit an imaginary situation, *e.g.*, the cardboard box becomes an airplane; she develops detailed scripts for imaginative play.

Play, Play and Play Some More!

Play – that pleasurable, spontaneous, active, creative, diverse thing your toddler does all day – is a direct route to learning. It may be fun, and it may seem like it's aimless or even foolish, but play is one of the keys to your child's cognitive, emotional and social development. Through play, she exercises her natural propensity to make the observations and associations that give words, objects and events their meaning. During the toddler stage, play falls into one of four main categories:

- **Locomotion Play:** Running, jumping, dancing.

- **Object Play:** Shaking, pulling and manipulating objects.

- **Social Play:** Physical games, such as wrestling with dad, and cooperative play, such as building a tower of blocks with a friend.

- **Imaginative Play:** Fitting objects and actions into fantasy situations – a uniquely human form of play.

Toddlers begin their second year with the more physical kinds of play and grow into the social and imaginative kinds of play. The changes happen over a period of about 14 months and during that time, innumerable lessons across a broad range of subjects are being learned.

Play Teaches Your Toddler About Herself and Others

A Sense of Mastery

It is through play that children first experience a feeling of mastery, both of the self and of objects. It's a great thrill for a toddler to know that she can make something happen. The confidence that comes from this feeling of mastery promotes further learning by motivating her to keep experimenting, observing and interacting with her world.

An Awareness of Emotions

Your toddler practices emotional awareness while she plays. It's hard to know what an emotion is until you've experienced what it feels like, and play enables toddlers to "try on" various feelings. She learns about anger and aggression when she kicks over her block tower and she learns about love and empathy when she feeds her stuffed animals. By about 21 months, as her autonomy and independence increase, she becomes extremely possessive

"...children's play...represents not only fun, but a critically important feature of their development of cognitive and emotional skills."
JEROME L. SINGER, DEVELOPMENTAL PSYCHOLOGIST

What's a Parent To Do?

ACTIVITY

On a sunny day, find a warm place in your driveway and do a shadow dance. Stand side-by-side with your toddler and raise your arm in the air. Have her look only at your shadow, and ask her to make the same shadow. Next move your other arm, your legs, your hips, etc.

BENEFIT

Demonstrates cause-and-effect relationships, develops body – and self-awareness and exercises both fine and gross motor skills.

about her playthings. The toys or objects are "mine" – they belong to this strong, powerful, emotional self that she has learned is "me."

A Sense of Belonging to a Social Unit

Play is one of the primary ways in which toddlers learn social and cultural rules:

- No one is happy when I hit my friend over the head with a fire truck.

- Everyone is happy when I let my friend share the tea set grandma gave me for my birthday.

Understanding Her Own and Other People's Actions

Understanding whether acts are intentional or accidental has an enormous impact on a toddler's ability to understand and predict the events in her world. The buzzing, whirring swirl of things that other people do, say and express starts to seem knowable – and separate from the things that the toddler herself does, says and feels.

"Once, during a large thunderstorm, my husband and I cuddled up with our twins, Aaron and Anthony. I asked the boys how they were doing and Aaron answered, 'Precious.' Confused by his response, I asked him why. He explained that he felt precious because he felt so loved being held and cuddled that way."

JOY PAGAZA, MOTHER OF AARON AND ANTHONY

Researchers call this insight into the thoughts, feelings and intentions of yourself and other people the "theory of mind." Knowing that you can make a decision and then take action to change the world, and knowing that other people can do the same is a huge cognitive leap forward. Through play, toddlers learn about the theory of mind. They take on roles, play by rules, imagine the life of other creatures – all of which relate directly to understanding their own and other's intentions. Recent findings indicate that toddlers' understanding about theory of mind is probably more advanced than we have ever given them credit for and has its beginnings sometime in the second year.

> **KEY-POINT**
> **"Toddlers use you as a role model and love to imitate your actions."**

How She Remembers and Imitates

Your toddler is constantly watching you and repeating what she observes. She might pick up a newspaper and mimic reading or grab the broom and imitate her older sister sweeping the dining room floor. Play enables her to

Supporting Evidence

Parents Serve as Good Role Models

Andrew Meltzoff, at the University of Washington, observed more than 200 14- and 16-month-old children to see if toddlers model their behavior after the adults around them. Dr. Meltzoff examined this issue by having some of the toddlers watch as an adult played with a toy for a total of one minute. To make sure he could tell when the child was imitating adult behavior rather than just playing with a toy in a natural way, Meltzoff had the adult do something a bit strange with the toy, such as tap his/her forehead on the toy. Some of the toddlers were allowed to play with the toy afterward, while others were not. A third group of toddlers was given the toy in a similar setting, but was never allowed to see the adult playing with the toy. Meltzoff had the toddlers return after both a two- and four-month period and gave them all the same toy — the one with which the adult had been playing. Even after this extended delay, all the toddlers who had watched the adult play with the toy imitated the adult behavior — even the toddlers who had not been given a chance to play with the toy the first time. Merely watching an adult for a total of just one minute, in other words, resulted in a strong learning and imitation pattern. The implications for parents are obvious: be sure to say "please" and "thank you" and be careful what you yell when you drop a can on your toe. Your toddler will imitate it all.

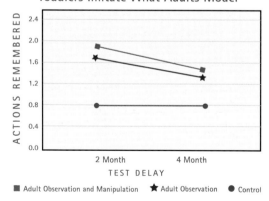

Toddlers Imitate What Adults Model

ACTIONS REMEMBERED (y-axis: 0.0, 0.4, 0.8, 1.2, 1.6, 2.0, 2.4)

TEST DELAY (x-axis: 2 Month, 4 Month)

■ Adult Observation and Manipulation ★ Adult Observation ● Control

Based upon data from Meltzoff, A.N. (1995). What Memory Tells Us About Infant Amnesia: Long-Term Recall and Deferred Imitation. *Journal of Experimental Child Psychology*, 59, 497-515.

pretend to do the important things the big people are doing. The amazing thing about the toddler is that her memory is growing stronger and stronger every day – which means that her ability to imitate is growing stronger, as well.

What Play Teaches Your Toddler About the Physical World

A Basic Understanding of the Physical World

Lessons about the solid and permanent nature of objects, the force of gravity and the ability of one action to cause a separate reaction are hardly lessons you would sit down and explain to a 15-month-old. But through observation and play, these are exactly what she is learning.

- Peek-a-boo is the perfect way to learn that things are still there even though you can't see them.

- Dropping things from your highchair to the floor eighteen times in a row is an ideal lesson in gravity – things never fall up.

- Pushing the button on the tape player and making music come out proves that by doing one thing, you can make another thing happen.

As part of her growing appreciation for the way the world works, your toddler gains a thorough understanding of the objects in her world. She becomes aware of the proper function for objects and tools, *e.g.*, the vacuum is for vacu-

Supporting Evidence

Is It Real or Is It A Photograph

How do we know that young children have difficulty separating symbols from real objects? Judy DeLoache and colleagues at the University of Illinois, Urbana-Champaign, asked whether children would treat a picture as if it were the actual object, or if they would treat a picture as if it were merely a symbol for the object itself. DeLoache had infants and toddlers, between 9- and 19-months of age look at pictures of things they were familiar with and then measured their response to the image. What she found was striking: young children – those under 19 months of age – treated the image as if it were the real object; they actually tried to pick it up and move it around. By 19 months, however, toddlers just pointed to the object. There was also an indication that increased exposure to symbols – in this case pictures – could accelerate the age at which a toddler was able to identify the symbol as a representation.

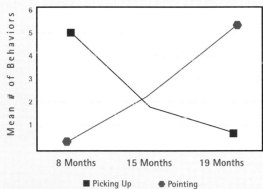

By 19 Months, Toddlers Know the Difference Between Pictures and Objects

Mean # of Behaviors

8 Months   15 Months   19 Months

■ Picking Up   ● Pointing

Based upon data taken from, DeLoache, J.S., Pierroutsakos, S.L. Uttal, D.H., Rosengren, K.S., and Gottlieb, A. (1998). Grasping the nature of pictures. *Psychological Science.* 9, 205-210.

uming, the cup is for drinking. Yet, between 12 and 18 months, as her imagination grows, she also invents new uses for familiar objects, playing with them in creative and novel ways.

The Meaning of Symbols

The major learning achievement of the period between 12 and 36 months is the transition from sensorimotor to representational thinking. Whereas a baby can only think of what she needs to feel good and what she sees in front of her, a toddler learns how to think of what she knows, what she remembers, what she can make happen and what she imagines. Scientists call this de-centered action as opposed to the self-centered actions of a baby, and it generally emerges around 19 months. At this time, your toddler begins to associate symbols that represent objects with the objects themselves:

"What the brain has done is lay out circuits that are its best guess about what's required for vision, for language, for whatever... and now it is up to neural activity — no longer spontaneous, but driven by a flood of sensory experiences — to take this rough blueprint and progressively refine it."

CARLA SHATZ, NEUROBIOLOGIST

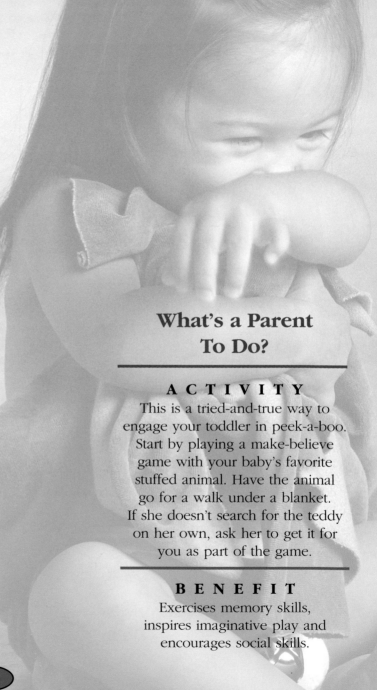

What's a Parent To Do?

ACTIVITY
This is a tried-and-true way to engage your toddler in peek-a-boo. Start by playing a make-believe game with your baby's favorite stuffed animal. Have the animal go for a walk under a blanket. If she doesn't search for the teddy on her own, ask her to get it for you as part of the game.

BENEFIT
Exercises memory skills, inspires imaginative play and encourages social skills.

- A funny-looking group of squiggly lines stands for a sound or a combination of sounds.

- That string of letters is not just a bunch of squiggly lines, but stands for a real word.

- A photograph of a cat is not the same thing as a real cat but is a representation of a real cat.

This is an enormous leap in cognitive development that opens up a whole new area of learning for your toddler. Suddenly she can play in a more symbolic or imaginative way. Encourage her in her efforts and join in on the fun, pretending to eat the soup she's cooked for lunch or cowering when she pretends she's a wolf. Some of the hallmarks of imaginative play include:

- Inanimate objects are treated as animate, *e.g.*, mothering a doll.

- Everyday activities are performed in the absence of the necessary materials, *e.g.*, drinking from an empty cup.

- The child performs actions that are usually done by someone else, *e.g.*, cooking, calling others on the "telephone."

- Activities are not carried out to their usual outcome, *e.g.*, grab the purse, grab the car keys, but do not go out and start the car.

- The object is substituted for another, *e.g.*, banana = phone.

- The child demonstrates affective behavior, *e.g.*, during a "distress scenario," children "fake cry" instead of actually crying.

Creating Categories

Human beings naturally want to group things. An abundance of evidence shows that even young infants can form categories. As your child matures, she can categorize objects as animate or inanimate and even categorize correctly when the similarity between objects is high, as between a bird and an airplane. By 14- to 22-months she can form categories based on smaller and more distinct features of things, which is why she may know the difference between a skip loader and a tractor.

Play enables your toddler to work on making groups of things according to what makes sense to her. She may sort her blocks by color, by shape, by function or by some other criteria. Being able to name objects and groups will help her make these categorical links, so be sure to name as many objects and categories as you can during your daily activities.

A Sense of Space and Time

During this year, your toddlers' sense of time and space grows and becomes an important aspect of her play:

- By 15 months of age, your toddler begins to have a more mature sense of space. She knows the meaning of "up" and "down" and can't get enough of peek-a-boo games.

- By 21 months, she understands space as a concrete concept: if a ball disappears behind the couch, she knows the ball exists and she knows it exists in a space behind the couch. This understanding of space leads her to enjoy rummaging through wastebaskets and the briefcase daddy left on the floor.

- Her notion of time is also expanding. She begins to understand the ideas of past, future and causality. She still lives primarily in the present, but she can now wait a minute for mom to pour her grape juice.

How To Play With Your Toddler

Just Do It

As adults we sometimes forget how to play, or forget the importance of play. Talk yourself into it if you have to, and get down on the floor to play with your toddler. There are literally hundreds of great ideas for games and activities in the **Ages and Stages** section at the back of this book. Pick the ones that work for you and play, play, play.

Know When to Stop

Too much of anything can do harm – even too much play. If your child is enjoying the toys and games you set out for her, keep on playing. But if she is getting fidgety, fussy or bored, take a break. Down time is just as important as play time for growing and learning.

Let Her Play Alone

Once you get into the habit of playing with your toddler it can be hard to stop. You think you always have to play with her. Remember that it's important for her to learn how to play by herself, to explore. Follow her lead or direct her to an activity, and then let her be.

Let Her Play At Her Own Pace

Some toddlers will play with a particular toy for so long that the parent assumes he is getting bored – or the parent

What's a Parent To Do?

ACTIVITY

Tape pictures of wild animals on the wall. Now take all of her stuffed animals, and place them under the pictures they match – the teddy bears beneath the grizzly bear, the elephants beneath the elephants and so on. Which picture ends up having the most stuffed animals?

BENEFIT

Reinforces sorting, counting and categorization skills.

is the one who gets bored. This is not necessarily the case. A shape sorter, for example, can be explored for how it looks, how it sounds, how it feels, how it rolls, how it fits into a basket – and this is all before the shapes are even brought into play. Let your toddler set the pace. She'll often give you signals that she's ready to do something else, and your job is simply to follow her lead.

Let Her Play With Friends

Although toddlers are just beginning to interact with their peers, it's still beneficial for them to be around each other. They learn so much by watching what other children do with a shovel or what the big kids do on the slide. They become familiar with the social rules that are expected of them. Small playgroups of three or four toddlers can be a great way to bring some social life into your toddler's world.

Buy Good Toys

Toys that are good for your toddler's development are smart purchases. Try to avoid toys that are meant to entice you rather than engage your child. Turn to our **Activities Toyguide** to learn which toys bring the most benefit for the longest period of time.

Keep Your Toys In Order

Toddlers can become overwhelmed by a room full of toys. Rotate the toys you set out for her, and keep the toys in boxes, bins, toy chests or bookshelves so that she can take out only the toys that interest her at the moment.

"If you grow up with lots of information processed, lots of opportunities for learning, you have a brain that is more complex, that has more wiring, [and] more connections between nerve cells."

WILLIAM T. GREENOUGH, NEUROBIOLOGIST

What's a Parent To Do?

A C T I V I T Y
Use a full deck of regular playing cards. Show your toddler how to sort them into piles by shape – such as diamonds and hearts. Later, you can make piles of red and black, and eventually, numbers.

B E N E F I T
A perfect lesson in color, shape and number concepts.

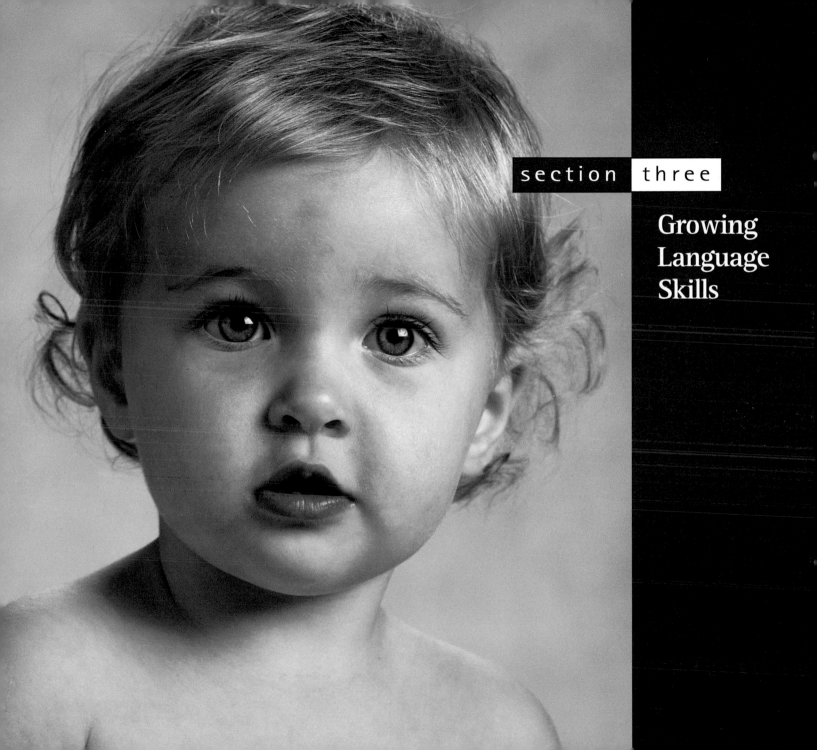

section three

Growing Language Skills

section three

Growing Language Skills

"The stimulation parents and other caregivers provide in the first three years sets the stage for effective, productive communication skills that will last a lifetime."

ROBERTA MICHNICK GOLINKOFF,
DEVELOPMENTAL PSYCHOLOGIST

What You'll Discover In This Section

- How language helps organize thought.

- How having conversations with your toddler can improve academic success throughout his lifetime.

- How your toddler can communicate with you by using gestures as well as words.

- How toddlers come to understand that strings of words make up a full thought.

"The individual's whole experience is built upon the plan of his language."

HENRI DELACROIX, AUTHOR

Language Organizes Thought

Between the ages of 12 and 24 months, most children become full-fledged talkers. They go from being able to utter a few simple words to successfully managing a vocabulary of more than a hundred words. By the age of two, many children can combine two words into simple sentences. Even those who aren't big talkers are mastering a full range of communication skills, from comprehending the words you say to gesturing for what they want. It's a thrilling transformation for parents and children alike, because communicating is one of those things that makes being human so rich, so rewarding and so much fun. It's also key, because language helps organize thought; it makes planning, counting, naming, creating categories of objects and storing memories all easier and more efficient.

What's especially exciting about language development is that it's one area where a parent's involvement can make a big difference. You couldn't do a thing to increase your child's ability to cut that first tooth or take that first step, but when it comes to talking, you can have a large and measurable impact.

Understanding Speech

Children understand words before they can say them. In fact, they can often understand complete sentences before they can speak even a handful of words. Many parents have great stories of how they first realized that their toddler understood more than they ever imagined – and, of course, they're often embarrassing. If you don't believe that

Key Milestones in Language Acquisition

Age	Milestone
12 to 15 Months	• Increases in Word Comprehension — he experiences a dramatic increase in the number of words he comprehends. • Use of Gestures — he continues to use gestures or to communicate, such as pointing to the refrigerator when he wants something to drink.
15 to 18 Months	• Nouns Prevalent — the vast majority of words he utters continue to be nouns, such as "ball," "mama" and "kitty." • Increased Phrase Comprehension — even though he's not producing multi-word sentences, he may begin to understand some aspects of multi-word speech.
18 to 21 Months	• Increased Word Production – he begins to add words to his production vocabulary at a great rate.
21 to 24 Months	• Simple Sentences — he begins to combine two words into simple sentences, such as "Me want." Later, he will add more words, such as to create more complex sentences. • Increased Use of Suffixes — he begins to add suffixes to indicate a plural or past tense, such as "puzzles" or "walked." • Over-Regularization-he begins to over — regularize (or inappropriately extend) linguistic rules, such as using "thinked" as the past tense of "think," or "mouses" for "mice."

your child's comprehension is greater than his speaking skills, ask him to do one of the following simple tasks:

• Place a ball on the floor and say, "Pick up the ball."

• When you get ready to change him say, "Bring me the diaper."

• As you build with blocks, say, "Hand me a block."

• Point to the toy box and ask your toddler to bring one block for you and another block for him.

• If he follows your one-step directions, try giving him a two-step task: "Please pick up the book and put it on the shelf."

• Place a ball and a duck on the floor near him and say, "Bring me the duck."

• As you build with red and yellow blocks, say, "Hand me the red block."

When toddlers get a little older, they love to hear mommy and daddy make deliberate mistakes in speech, particularly in familiar songs and nursery rhymes:

• Try singing, 'Twinkle, twinkle little rocket ship,' and you're sure to get a joyous protest from your audience.

• Admit your mistake and sing, 'Twinkle, twinkle little bulldozer,' and the crowd may just roll in the aisles.

Parents tell it like it is:

"We'd been reading board books to Steven since he was about two months old, always wondering if he was getting anything out of it. One day, when Steven was about 13 months old, my husband turned on a basketball game. Steven ran and got one of his 'shapes' books, pointed to it, then pointed to the television, and said, "ball." At that moment, we knew that all the time we spent reading was, in fact, paying off."

GRACE MORI, MOTHER OF STEVEN

Understanding More Speech: Memory and Word Retention

A big leap in the ability to comprehend words happens around the end of the first year when children are able to remember words for longer periods of time. They can now clearly understand words that are not being used in relation to a particular object. If, for example, you're on the way home from the grocery store, and you say, "I'm going

Supporting Evidence

Beginning Speakers Begin To Comprehend Complex Sentences

Kathy Hirsh-Pasek, of Temple University, and Roberta Michnick Golinkoff, of the University of Delaware, conducted an ingenious study to examine toddler's understanding of how words are combined into sentences. The researchers had toddlers ages 12- to 15- months view one of two nonsensical images on a television screen: an image of a woman kissing keys or an image of a woman kissing a ball. The toddlers then heard a voice say, "She's kissing the keys." Hirsh-Pasek and Golinkoff reasoned that if the toddlers understood only a portion of the sentence, they would have no preference for which screen to look at. If, however, they understood the details of the sentence, they would look longer at the screen whose image matched the voice-over. The toddlers did, in fact, spend more time looking at the screen where the woman was kissing the keys.

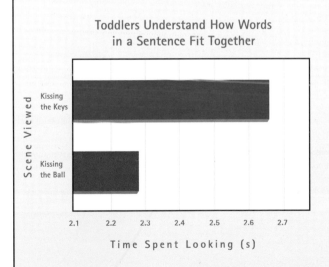

Toddlers Understand How Words in a Sentence Fit Together

Scene Viewed

Kissing the Keys

Kissing the Ball

2.1 2.2 2.3 2.4 2.5 2.6 2.7

Time Spent Looking (s)

Based upon data presented in Hirsh-Pasek, K., and Golinkoff, R.M. (1999). *The Origins of Grammar: Evidence from Early Language Comprehension*. Cambridge: MIT Press.

to make peanut butter and jelly sandwiches for lunch," your toddler can understand what he'll be having for lunch even though there is no peanut butter and jelly within sight.

Children even begin to understand out-of-context words that they are not able to say. You may not know he has this skill, of course, but it's there all the same. If you visit the zoo, for example, and you point to a flamingo and tell your toddler that he's looking at a flamingo, he may not be able to say 'flamingo' but he can remember the funny pink bird with the funny word that describes it. As his oral-motor skills develop he may surprise you one day by pointing to a billboard covered in flamingos and saying 'flamingo' even though he hasn't heard the word or seen the animal since the visit to the zoo. Because repetition helps children hold words in their memory, say new words such as 'flamingo' (or 'entrance' or 'wheelbarrow') as many times as you can, and point to what you're talking about as often as you can.

KEY-POINT
"Toddlers can understand many more words than they can produce."

The Language of Gesture

Children of this age rely on a rather extensive set of gestures to get their caregivers to give them what they need and want. If you watch a young toddler for even a short period of time, you'll see him making a wide range of deliberate motions, each of which probably means one specific thing.

- Lifting his hands up may mean: "I want to be picked up."

- Pointing at the refrigerator may mean: "I'd like juice."

- Walking to his shelves, pulling out a book and handing it to you may mean: "This is one of my favorite books, and I would like you to read it to me now" – which is a rather complex and organized set of ideas.

Although these are gestures every one-year-old uses, each child has invented it all on his own. Some children invent more gestures than others. Often, these are the children who will start talking sooner. They just seem to have a stronger need to communicate and are eager to replace their reaching and pointing with appropriate words.

What's a Parent To Do?

ACTIVITY

As you sing "Old MacDonald Had a Farm" walk around like the animals in the song. Try strutting like a rooster and stamping your foot like a horse.

BENEFIT

Develops singing and language skills, inspires imaginative play and teaches body control.

Signs of Language Impairment

Noticing your toddler's efforts at gesturing is an important observation, not only for understanding what he is trying to communicate but also for catching any developmental delays as early as possible. When combined with extreme delays in verbal production an inability for your toddler to communicate via gestures can be a sign of a long-term language deficit. These kinds of deficits are very responsive to early intervention, so the earlier they are noted, tracked and addressed, the better. (See checkpoints in our **Assessment** section, page 89.)

Parents of boys should note that boys are more vulnerable to language impairment than girls. Boys also tend to lag behind girls in their speech production. It can be easy, therefore, to assume that a male child who is 24- months-old and is not talking is just a late bloomer. Such an assumption, however, is a mistake. Lack of gesturing, especially when it's combined with lack of speech production, should never be ignored. An inability to hold your gaze is also associated with delays in language. If your child is not speaking by the age of two, no matter boy or girl, and no matter what the other signs, be sure to ask your pediatrician for a complete hearing test.

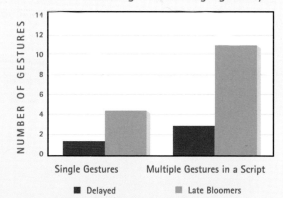

Speech Begins in Earnest

Getting to Word One

Learning to speak distinct words with actual meanings is a complex process and no two children go about it in exactly the same way. Your child may quickly move from babbling to talking by the end of his first year, or he may not begin speaking distinct words until the end of the second year. Both paths are natural and appropriate ways to becoming a communicator. One way to help your baby learn to speak, no matter what his learning style, is to name the objects your child comes into contact with throughout the day. Even if it seems as if your toddler is not paying attention, rest assured that he's taking it all in. As long as he shows no signs of developmental delay (see **Assessment**, page 85), sit tight and keep talking. He'll talk back soon enough.

"...language is absolutely central to the development of intelligence and social skills."

BURTON L. WHITE, PARENTING EXPERT

Talking to a Brick Wall?

For some parents talking to a baby is the most natural thing in the world. These people prattle on all day about the hat the neighbor is wearing and the song playing on the ice cream truck. For other parents, talking to someone who can't talk back, who may not even look at you when you talk, and who doesn't appear to understand what you're saying, simply feels ridiculous – like talking to a brick wall. If you're not a natural talker, don't feel you have to jump in and start narrating every move you make throughout the day. Start by focusing on what you and your toddler are doing and describe it out loud:

KEY-POINT
"Many long-term benefits come from speaking frequently to your toddler."

> **"I've got your bath ready."**
> **"I'm going to get your dinner now."**
> **"We need to go to the store."**

Talking about what you are going to do, and then doing it, helps your toddler connect words with actions. Simply hearing your voice helps him to begin producing words himself. You'll probably find yourself talking more and more easily with every passing day. The results of this increase can be staggering. Studies have shown that an increase in toddler-directed talk does far more than build a bigger vocabulary or a more confident communicator; it results in an increase in everything from academic performance to IQ.

What's a Parent To Do?

ACTIVITY

Create a ritual around dressing time by explaining your choice of clothes. "We'll wear this sweater today because it is going to be 'cold.'" "We are going to wear the fancy shirt today because we are going to a 'formal' party."

BENEFIT

Builds vocabulary and helps them understand the relationship between the weather and what you wear.

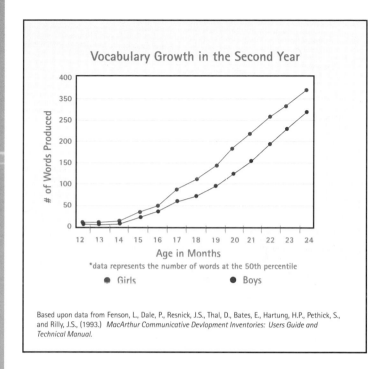

Vocabulary Growth in the Second Year

*data represents the number of words at the 50th percentile

● Girls   ● Boys

Based upon data from Fenson, L., Dale, P., Resnick, J.S., Thal, D., Bates, E., Hartung, H.P., Pethick, S., and Rilly, J.S., (1993.) *MacArthur Communicative Devlopment Inventories: Users Guide and Technical Manual.*

Vocabulary Spurts

Learning to speak is not just about knowing what words to say. It's also about forming those words with the tongue, the lips and the mouth. In order to speak, you need both the physical ability to form the words and the brain development necessary to know when to use them. As children grow, they not only learn more words but their oral-motor skills also improve so they can say more words.

Toddler-Directed Talk Predicts Academic Success

In the early 1960s, Betty Hart and Todd R. Risley, researchers at the University of Kansas, embarked on an ambitious research study. They tracked the day-to-day activities of one- and two-year-olds in their homes and examined the impact these environments had on later academic achievement. For over two years, observers spent one hour per month in the homes of 42 families, recording as much detail about their interactions as possible. They recorded such things as the amount of baby-directed talking, the type of talking and the tone the parents used with their children, each of which varied widely from household to household. The result of their efforts is one of the most comprehensive studies ever conducted detailing the communication patterns that parents share with their children and how these patterns affected the later academic performance of their children.

Hart and Risley kept track of these children through fifth grade, cross-referencing their early findings against later academic performance. What they learned was that one of the key predictors of academic performance was the amount of talking that was directed at the baby. In some households there was a great deal of stimulation, such as books, toys, outings and infant-directed talk. The children raised in these households enjoyed later academic success. While it is difficult to isolate individual aspects of such an enriched environment, it was clear from the Hart and Risley study that baby-directed talk — one of the cheapest, easiest and most natural activities — was an important component of the environment.

"A word is not a crystal, transparent and unchanging, it is the skin of a living thought and may vary greatly in color and content according to the circumstances and time in which it is used."

OLIVER WENDELL HOLMES, JR., AUTHOR

• Often following a burst in word comprehension, many children will experience great bursts of language learning. In just a short time, they'll learn anywhere from 10 to 40 new words.

> **KEY-POINT**
> *"Many toddlers experience a vocabulary spurt at around 18 months."*

• Other children learn more gradually. They may never experience a big vocabulary burst, but they are still acquiring new words all the time.

Predictors of Language Development

When and how much your toddler speaks is often a point of comparison among parents. It's no wonder, because speech is such an obvious and exciting development. There are many factors that affect the development of language. Some of these are under your control and include:

• **Amount of Toddler-Directed Speech**

   In addition to the findings produced by Hart and Risley, Janellen Huttenlocher, at the University of Chicago, has found that not only does the amount of baby-directed speech in a household predict vocabulary growth, she has also found that it affects the rate at which toddlers develop increasingly complex forms of grammar and syntax.

- **Type of Toddler-Directed Speech**

  Researchers have found that toddlers tend to speak earlier if their parents tend to use more concrete, object-oriented speech, such as "Look at the wind moving the trees," or "I see that you liked your macaroni and cheese; it's all gone!" rather than "It's windy," or "You were hungry today."

Some of these are not under your control and include:

- **Birth Order**

  Researchers have found evidence that birth order plays a part in which children have vocabulary spurts and which do not. The theory is that first-born children tend to receive more one-on-one attention from their parents and, as a result, are part of a lot more high-quality conversations. What's clear is that whether your toddler is your first child or your fifth, the more you talk to him in a direct and responsive manner, the more words he is hearing and storing away to use himself.

- **Gender**

  No matter what birth order they are in, or how responsive their parents are in the way they talk, girls tend to produce and understand words earlier than boys. The difference is only slight, and no one knows the reasons for it, but we see this result time and again.

- **Personality**

  Personality may also affect how fast your child learns words. Children who smile and laugh a great deal, and who are easily calmed by their mothers, tend to learn more words at an earlier age. This may be because children who don't need to put a lot of effort into calming themselves have more energy to dedicate to other tasks, like learning language.

"My words fly up, my thoughts remain below. Words without thoughts never to heaven go."

From Words to Sentences

Frozen Phrases

At about two years of age, most children begin to put two words together in phrases that sound like simple sentences. These phrases may sound like a two-word sentence, but they are, in fact, being used as one word. Researchers call these early expressions "frozen phrases" because children are using them as if they were one word:

- Your child might say "whatsat," which sounds to an adult like "what's that," but he can't separate "what" from "that" in any functional way. He thinks these two words are inseparable. He is unable to make the shift to say, "what's this."

In time, children learn the separate and distinct words "more" and "go," and learn how to apply the concepts to anything – more juice, more toast, more jelly beans. These later phrases may sound just like the frozen phrases, but they are, in fact, much closer to being a true sentence.

Supporting Evidence

Early Sentence Formation

Developmental psychologist Roger Brown pioneered the concept that early sentences are based on 'peg words' – one word that serves as a peg around which a child rotates other words. If 'more' is the peg word, for example, 'banana' or 'apple' are the add-ons. This results in phrases such as 'more apple' and 'more banana.' But is 'more apple' a sentence? Julian Pine and Elena Lieven, at the University of Manchester, have examined this question by following a group of toddlers over an eight-month period, starting at age one. What they found was that many of a toddler's first sentences are not true sentences at all; instead, toddlers are combining the sounds of two words to create a 'master' word, or a frozen phrase. The researchers found that instead of using each part of the frozen phrase to form additional phrases, most toddlers go back, learn each word all over again, and then learn how to use it as a peg in a true sentence.

Until he gets to that stage, keep stressing individual words and using them in a wide variety of contexts. When he says 'more milk,' ask him if he would also like more crackers or more peas. Later in the day, say, 'Look, there are more kids walking home from school.'

Grasping Grammar

Using correct grammar is a skill that is way beyond children who are learning how to speak. Some researchers believe that children are able to recognize when incorrect grammar is being used. In one study, for example, children recognized when the subject and object in a sentence were switched, but even so, they had no understanding of the grammatical structure itself. Applying proper grammar skills to speech is the last step in the process of being able to carry out complex communications.

As a child learns more words he will begin to make fewer and fewer mistakes. You can help him by echoing his mistakes with the correct grammatical structure. When he says, "Daddy don't like chocolate," say, "You're right, daddy doesn't like chocolate." He'll quickly get the point.

Building Your Toddler's Communication Skills

- **Listen and Respond**

  It's important to talk to your child, but it's also important to listen. As your child attempts to talk, listen carefully to what he's saying (or trying to say) and repeat his words back to him as if you're having a conversation.

- **Join in His Play**

  Doing an activity together and talking about it is a natural way to increase your child's vocabulary and command of his language. Building blocks, for example, give you the chance to use words such as build, place, put, up, down, more, another, long, short, high, low, balance, bridge, tower, skyscraper, etc.

- **Let Him Take the Lead**

  Help set the stage for play only as much as you need to; let him take the lead, choosing the game and its rules, and let him be as creative as he wants to be.

- **Model Correct Usage**

  If you consistently use correct grammar, your child will eventually use it, as well. Remember that toddlers are great imitators. If he does make a big mistake, explain the mistake and reinforce the correct words. For example, if you hold up a doll and he says, "ball," you might say, "Almost! That's not a ball; it's a doll. D-d-doll."

- **Ask Questions**

  To help your child increase his powers of communication, ask him specific questions and encourage him to try again. Questions such as, "You want me to put the ball where?" are far more encouraging than questions such as "What did you say?"

- **Let Him Work for It**

  Don't jump in too quickly when someone outside the family doesn't understand what your child is saying. Let him attempt to communicate; it's good practice.

What's a Parent To Do?

ACTIVITY

While having lunch, talk about the bananas, peas and apples. Describe the taste and texture, (*e.g.*, sweet or sour, crunchy or soft.) This is an especially good time to compare and contrast.

BENEFIT

Introduces new words and concepts.

Parents tell it like it is:

"I was having a fancy dinner party and took out our nice crystal and china – something I almost never do. Emily was 18 months old, and I kept telling her, "Don't touch! They're fragile."
I couldn't think of a better word to say than 'fragile,' so I just kept saying it, hoping she'd get the idea.
When the guests finally arrived, she came out to say goodnight, pointed at a tea cup and told everyone not to touch it because it was fragile. All the guests were amazed at her brilliant vocabulary, but I'm sure that all she was doing was repeating what she heard me say a dozen times."

JENNIE ROBERTSON, MOTHER OF EMILY AND CARLYN

section four

Pre-Literacy

Pre-Literacy

"Happy is he who has laid up in his youth, and held fast in all fortune, a genuine and passionate love of reading."

RUFUS CHOATE, LAWYER

What You'll Discover In This Section

- How literacy develops as a result of the way you talk, play, read and interact with your toddler.

- The many benefits of story time.

- How you serve as a reading role model.

- How to lay the foundation for a love of reading.

"Man reading should be man intensely alive. The book should be a ball of light in one's hand."

EZRA POUND, POET

Reading Foundations

Reading isn't something that happens all at once, like magic – voilà, your child is flipping through "War and Peace." Literacy is a process your toddler has been learning all her life, and largely from you; this is why scientists refer to the process as emergent literacy. Literacy develops as you sit with her to read a picture book, put together an alphabet puzzle or sound out words together. Scientists consider literacy to be the process of acquiring the skills to both read and write. It is a gradual process of development that begins with listening and babbling and continues throughout a lifetime of reading pleasure.

KEY-POINT
"Seemingly small gains in understanding letters and sounds contribute to the development of literacy."

Because literacy happens over time, all the reading experiences you provide for your toddler lay the foundation for excellence in literacy for the rest of her life. Your toddler is very interested in sounds and words; her vocabulary is growing, and she is instinctively imitating your behaviors. This is a great time to begin introducing her to language and to the written word.

Storytime

For toddlers, literacy grows and blossoms at story time. The simple act of reading stories aloud to your toddler is like a graduate course in the way words work. Each time you read a story out loud, you are exposing your toddler to oral and written language and you are demonstrating that reading is a pleasurable experience – after all, she gets to sit close to you and hear the comforting sound of your voice.

Key Milestones in Pre-Literacy

Age	Milestone
12 to 15 Months	• Differentiates the Sounds of Language — she clearly differentiates the sounds that make up her native language, and begins to have more difficulty differentiating the sounds from other languages. • Holds a Book — she holds books in both hands, although not always with the book in the correct orientation. • Turns Pages — she turns the pages of books, although not always in the appropriate left-to-right direction.
15 to 18 Months	• Learns Print Conventions — she begins to understand the conventions of print, *e.g.*, the pages are flipped from left to right, the first word is at the top of the page, etc.
18 to 21 Months	• Links Letters With Their Sounds — she begins to link letters to the sounds they represent. • Recognizes Symbols — she begins to recognize objects in books, and begins to understand that they represent objects in the real world.
21 to 24 Months	• Holds a Book Correctly — she continues to hold a book in both hands, but is now developing a sense of correct orientation. • Recognizes One or Two Letters — she begins to recognize a few letters, most notably, the first letter of her name.

Recent studies have found evidence that the amount of literacy opportunities a child has at home has a direct effect on how strong her language abilities will be as a preschooler. In fact, in one study of a group of two-year olds, researchers discovered that a significant percent of their speech each day occurred during story time. If you've already started a habit of reading to your child, you can now increase the time you spend on it. You can also add new books with more words and more complex stories. If you haven't made reading a part of your life, you can jump in with both feet now. Below, we list dozens of ideas for making story time fun, making it stick and making it work. In our **Ages and Stages** sections, we also recommend hundreds of excellent books.

> **KEY-POINT**
> "A daily story time ritual provides your toddler benefits ranging from emotional closeness to a love of reading."

How to make story time a part of your daily life

- Just as you try to set consistent times for naps, baths and bedtime, choose a special time to read to your child. She'll look forward to the chance to be close to you, to listen to your voice and to share a few unhurried moments.

- Find a comfortable spot where you can sit together and look at the pages as you read. A couch, a big chair or a pile of pillows on the floor are all great choices.

What's a Parent To Do?

A C T I V I T Y

Pull your toddler onto your lap, and instead of reading her a children's book, read her what *you* want to read – the newspaper, a magazine, a recipe, a letter from a friend, etc. Point to the pictures and the cartoons as you go.

B E N E F I T

Builds pre-literacy skills – including a love of reading – and encourages social skills.

- Keep reading time short at first – just a few minutes is enough – then gradually increase it as your toddler's attention span gets longer.

- If your toddler starts to wiggle and squirm or seems more interested in reaching for a toy across the room from you, it's probably time to stop reading. You want reading time to be something she looks forward to, not something from which she tries to escape.

- Create a simple ritual at the end of story time, such as saying, "That was a great book," and then putting the book back on the shelf.

- Keep a list of favorite books and authors in your toddler's memory book.

Parents tell it like it is:

"When my youngest child was a year-and-a-half, my oldest child was learning how to read. There were books everywhere, we read constantly and we made frequent trips to the library. We didn't even think about the impact on the younger child, but she began taking certain books to bed and tucking them under the covers, as if they were favorite stuffed animals. She's only three-and-a-half now, and begging to learn how to read."
JENNIE ROBERTSON, MOTHER OF CARLYN AND EMILY

How to make story time fun

- Make reading aloud a family activity. Let mom, dad or older sisters and brothers take turns reading to your toddler.

- Point to the pictures and name the objects and characters.

- Use books that encourage interaction. Textures, pull-down flaps and pop-up illustrations reinforce literacy skills and help make reading fun.

- Use a lively, animated tone of voice as you act out the dialogue of the main character in the story.

- Create anticipation as you read by making comments such as, "I wonder what will happen next?"

- Choose books that feature a funny character, a clever rhyme or beautiful pictures. You'll find suggestions for appropriate books in the **Ages and Stages** sections. Don't forget the books you loved as a child. It can be a wonderful tradition to share the same books with your child that your parents read to you.

How to make story time effective

- Read slowly and respond to whatever your child seems to find most interesting in the story.

- Encourage her to 'read' with you. Once she knows the book by heart, let her finish a sentence for you. This helps her to learn that the written words have meaning.

- Let her handle the pages and gently turn them, and point out to her where you are on a page.

- Teach her to look at the pictures; they often help to tell the story and show her what is coming next.

- When she is ready, let her 'echo' read with you. You read a short sentence and she says it back to you.

- Try talking about the story as you ask about the colors of the pictures, the shapes on the page or whatever seems to capture her interest.

Repetition Builds Knowledge

Repetition is very important for children at this age. Your child may ask you to read the same book twice in a row, or bring it to you to read every day. Although it can be hard to understand why she wants to hear the same story so many times, there are good reasons why children enjoy this kind of repetition. Not only do they find it comforting to hear familiar stories, but hearing words and phrases repeated helps to lay the foundation for reading comprehension.

Beyond Story Time

Reading stories to your toddler is important, but it's not all you can do. Here are some other ideas for bringing literacy into your toddler's life.

- **Become a Reading Role Model**

  Children at this age are very aware of what their parents do. They model their own actions and play on what they see mom or dad doing and imitate your everyday activities, such as driving a car, going shopping and working on the computer. To make reading a part of your child's life, let her see that reading is a part of yours. She'll naturally want to imitate it. Explain what you're doing when you read a recipe, a cereal box, the newspaper and the mail. Give her a book to look at when you sit down to read a magazine and say, "Let's read for a few minutes." Researchers agree that exposure to reading in the home is a very important part of preparing a child to read on her own.

  KEY-POINT
  "Making your reading time an interactive experience enhances your toddler's understanding of the conventions of reading."

"Books are the quietest and most constant of friends; they are the most accessible and wisest of counselors, and the most patient of teachers."
CHARLES W. ELIOT, AUTHOR

Supporting Evidence

Participation in the Reading Experience

Grover Whitehurst and his colleagues at the University of New York at Stonybrook, have created an approach to reading that increases a toddler's involvement in the experience. They worked with two- and three-year-olds enrolled in Head-Start programs. The process Whitehurst developed, which he refers to as "Dialogic Reading," involves having parents ask toddlers questions about reading. Questioning focuses on individual pages, asking toddlers to describe what they are seeing on the page, and what is happening on the page. Parents are also encouraged to add information about what is happening in the story. In a recent study, Whitehurst found that this type of reading has a significant impact on a toddler's understanding of the reading materials, and the conventions of reading. Whitehurst and his colleagues worked with 167 four-year-old children over the course of a year; 94 of these children received special dialogic reading experiences – both at home and in school; the remaining 73 children received their standard reading experiences. Children in the dialogic reading group scored higher in many areas of literacy. For example, they experienced a 93 percent increase in their ability to link words and sounds – a critical pre-literacy skill.

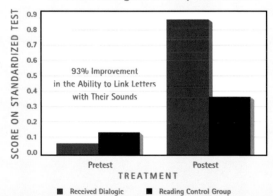

Actively Engaging Your Toddler in Reading Leads to Better Emergent Literacy Performance

93% Improvement in the Ability to Link Letters with Their Sounds

Y-axis: SCORE ON STANDARDIZED TEST (0.0–0.9)
X-axis: TREATMENT (Pretest, Postest)
Legend: ■ Received Dialogic ■ Reading Control Group

Based upon data from Whitehurst, G.J., Epstein, J.N., Angell, A., Payne, A.C., Crone, D., & Fischel, J.E. (1994). Outcomes of an emergent literacy intervention in Head Start. *Journal of Educational Psychology, 84*, 541-556.

- **Create a Library**

Integrate books and printed material into your toddler's play areas. Fill a small bookcase with board books she can remove, read and replace herself. If you have enough shelf space, display the books so that the covers face forward; if not, place a few books out on a coffee table. If her favorite place to play is a pretend kitchen, you might put some empty cereal boxes or milk cartons where she can see and reach them. Add recipes, grocery lists and menus. If she prefers to build things with a carpentry set, add some instruction manuals or draw some pretend blueprints and tape them up. The point is to begin showing her that reading is a part of her world and to give her the chance to combine play with reading. You want to add printed materials to her play spaces and then play with her, giving her ideas about how she can use the printed materials as she plays. Whenever you see her pretending to read, encourage the behavior.

> **KEY-POINT**
> "Creating an enriched literary environment, by making books easily accessible for your toddler, fosters a long-term interest in reading."

- **Sign Up for Story Time**

Your toddler may be ready for a lap-sit story time session at your local bookstore or library. Many libraries hold these special sessions geared for children starting around age two. The stories tend to be short ones that will hold a child's attention. Attending story times like these can be a nice change of pace and can help make reading seem extra special. In addition, it provides an early form of social interaction in a non-threatening setting. Your toddler is not yet ready for shared play, but she can have the experience of sharing reading with other children while still having you close at hand.

Parents tell it like it is:

"Whenever Kira sees a 'K' – whether it's on a billboard or a box – we have to stop so she can point, and spell her name, K,K,K,K,K, I, r, a."

JEFF HOUSMAN, FATHER OF KIRA AND LEAH

"If the riches of the Indies, or the crowns of all the kingdom of Europe, were laid at my feet in exchange for my love of reading, I would spurn them all."

FRANCOIS FENELON, AUTHOR

- **Make the Library Part of Your Routine**

  Once a month, or more often if you can manage it, go to the library to look at the books. Pull a few picture books off the shelf to read while you're at the library, then let your toddler pick a few to take home. Many libraries have boxes into which a toddler can dig for board books. At home, create a special library book box where these borrowed books are kept. When it's time to return the books, let your toddler put them into the library return slot before she picks out a few more to take home. This active involvement with a wide range of books is a great pre-literacy routine.

Supporting Evidence

How Reading Aloud Affects Literacy Skills

Adriana Bus and colleagues at Leiden University in the Netherlands have recently conducted a full review of the literature regarding how parents' reading to their children affects later measures of literacy. This type of analysis is referred to as a "meta-analysis," because its purpose is to study the results of a wide range of studies. Bus looked at a number of measures of reading and overall language ability, such as early literacy skills, long-term reading achievement and overall language skills. The results were very clear, as the chart below shows: across each of these measures, there is a very strong relationship between reading to children and language and reading skills.

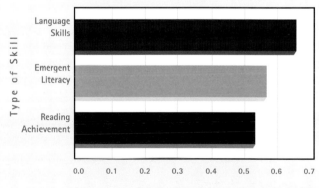

Reading to Your Toddler Improves Reading and Language Skills

Type of Skill: Language Skills, Emergent Literacy, Reading Achievement

Strength of Relationship to Book Reading

0.0 0.1 0.2 0.3 0.4 0.5 0.6 0.7

Based upon data from Bus, A.G., Ijzendoorn, M.H., & Pelligrini, A. (1995). Joint Book reading makes for success in learning to read: A meta-analysis on intergenerational transmission of literacy. Review of Educational Research, 65, 1-21.

What's a Parent To Do?

A C T I V I T Y

On the outside of your child's dresser, place a picture of the various items that go in the drawers. Label each picture with a word that describes the item. When it's time to get dressed, ask him where the socks (or underwear or a shirt) are.

B E N E F I T

Builds pre-literacy skills and encourages both memory and independence.

Parents tell it like it is:

"We read to our twins, Ashley and Andrea, all the time, and I love the way reading enters into their play. I overheard Andrea talking on her toy phone, saying, 'Grandma, hello. Hello. Do you like my hat? I do not like it. Good-bye. Good-bye.' This just so happens to be a line from one of their favorite books, 'Go, Dog Go!,' by P.D. Eastman."

MICHELLE FRANCO

MOTHER OF ALICIA, ASHLEY AND ANDREA

section five

Social and Emotional Development

Social and Emotional Development

What You'll Discover | In This Section

"It is the responsibility of every adult
to make sure that children hear
what we have learned from the lessons of life and to
hear over and over that we love them
and that they are not alone."

MARIAN WRIGHT EDELMAN,
FOUNDER OF THE CHILDREN'S DEFENSE FUND

- How social interactions lead to advances in your toddler's intellectual capabilities.

- How your toddler develops selfhood and autonomy.

- The importance of your toddler's experiments and explorations.

- How your toddler learns society's rules.

- How language development affects emotional and intellectual development.

"Everyone is born with the capacity for empathy...it's part of our biological and cognitive wiring. But there is also a lot of social scaffolding and experiences that can influence how empathy develops, which means we can do something about it."

JANET STRAYER, PH.D., PSYCHOLOGIST

We live in a social and emotional world. One of the major roles a parent plays, especially during the first few years of life, is creating an environment in which children can feel safe, in which they can explore and in which they can flourish. Although we think of social interactions and emotional control as separate from intellectual development, many of the advances we see in social and emotional development in the second year of life are directly related to intellectual advances. In many cases – such as your toddler's awareness that he is a separate and unique individual with the power to change the world – advances in social and emotional development create advances in intellectual development.

The emotional and social advances of the second year all occur in relation and in reaction to parents and caregivers. The interaction your toddler has with you and the feedback he gets from you are the fuel he needs to develop a sense of self, learn the rules of his society and venture out into the world on his own. Love, trust and respect, in other words, are helping your toddler's brain reach its fullest intellectual potential.

Becoming an Individual

As almost any parents who have been through the process before can tell you, one of the primary advances your toddler makes is learning that he is a separate and unique individual. This is a process that developmental specialists refer to as individuation. It is a process that encompasses growth in many areas of development, including emotional, social and intellectual.

• It All Starts With a Secure Attachment

A strong bond with a loving caregiver provides the trust and confidence your toddler needs to explore the world. Toddlers depend on their parents to give them cues about how to make their way in the world, and how to react to their surroundings. It is through your consistent,

Key Milestones in Emotional Growth

Age	Milestone
12 to 15 Months	• Enjoys Success — through repeated experience, he develops a sense of mastery and control of things in his environment. • Understands and Tests Limits — as he develops a sense of independence, he tests the limits set by parents and caregivers. • Cautious Exploration — he begins to explore his surroundings, but checks that a caregiver is nearby. • Increasing Negativism — he can easily become irritable as he faces the do's and don'ts of the social world.
15 to 18 Months	• Sense of Physical Self — he develops an increasing awareness of his body. • Develops a Sense of Self — his sense of self and identity is beginning to emerge. • Seeks Help in Regulating Emotion — he will look to you to help regulate his emotions when faced with unknown or challenging situations. • Transitional Objects — he is able to use a transitional object, such as a "blankie," to provide comfort.
18 to 21 Months	• Understanding Social Conventions — he begins to focus on the way things "should be" and on what is "normal." • Pro-Social Behavior — he engages in pro-social behavior when someone else is distressed, e.g., gives mom a truck when she hurts her foot. • Developing Peer Interactions — although full-fledged play interactions are still a way off, he begins to understand that another person can be a useful part of play. • Seeks Autonomy — his increased sense of selfhood can sometimes result in increased negative attitude and behavior.
21 to 24 Months	• Defines Emotions With Words — he continues to identify and define his emotions by using words. • Expresses Emotions — he begins to use language to express how he is feeling emotionally. • Develops Complex Emotions — he shows the first signs of complex emotions, such as pride, shame and guilt. • Develops Appropriate Pro-Social Behaviors — he continues to act pro-socially, but does so in a more appropriate way, e.g., gets mom a bandage when she hurts her foot. • Pride in Achievement — he not only shows pride and pleasure in his achievements, he also checks to see if others have noticed.

caring presence that your toddler begins to gain a sense of himself and of others. Many experts believe that early attachment has an impact on the relationships a toddler will form throughout his life, but they also believe early attachment impacts intellectual skills.

- **Separation Anxiety Is a Normal Part of the Process**

Although it can be hard to live through, separation anxiety is a positive step in your toddler's development. Your toddler knows he is separate from you – in both mind and body – and knows that he depends on the emotional cues he gets from you to decide how to react. Reassure him that you will return, and if he hasn't already chosen one for himself, find a comforting transitional object, such as a picture of yourself or even a piece of your clothing, to help him regulate his emotions in your absence.

> **KEY-POINT**
> "A trusting relationship with your toddler provides the security he needs to confidently explore his environment, and hence, to learn."

You can also take comfort from the fact that this anxiety will subside over time. Between 18- and 30-months, toddlers separate more easily. This change is due to an increased understanding that you are a permanent part of his world: you exist, even when you're not right in front of him, and you always come back after you've left. By this time, he is also becoming more adept at regulating his own emotions.

- **The Age of Exploration Begins**

A growing sense of autonomy is a big milestone in the second year of development. You can see it as your toddler becomes less clingy, and more willing to explore his environment on his own. He may head up the stairs by himself, or open the bottom drawer and pull everything out. He'll also become interested in naming and touching his own body parts – a perfect exercise in self-definition. Make sure the environment is safe for exploration, and applaud all his efforts at self-reliance.

- **Interaction With Others Increases**

Toddlers love to imitate and initiate behavior – laughing to make you laugh, or joining in a song that someone else has started singing. They have not only figured out that experiences can be shared with other people, but also that certain behaviors produce certain emotions, and vice versa. This discovery is often the start of extreme emotional displays, such as heartfelt hugs and angry pouts.

- **Communication Gets More Complex**

  Once your toddler knows that information and emotions can be communicated, he'll begin to communicate through a combination of increasingly complex emotions, gestures and speech. He'll tell you when he's sad, or if you've hurt his feelings. Helping him communicate these emotions is a great way to helping him be able to regulate these feelings even when you're not there.

There is evidence that an evolved sense of self is also related to an ability to communicate with empathy toward others. Toddlers with a mature sense of self are more likely to empathize when someone else shows signs of distress.

- **Defiance and Negativity Are a Normal Part of the Process**

  Recognizing that you are separate from others leads to feelings of defiance, negativism and sometimes, even aggressive behavior. If your son heads for the shiny doorknob after you told him not to, or if he refuses to undress and get in his ducky pajamas, remember this is age-appropriate behavior. If he hits or pushes a child who wants his toy (screaming, "mine, mine"), don't be too alarmed. Kindly and firmly remove him from the situation and redirect his attention. Be patient and consistent – learning these lessons can sometimes take a while.

KEY-POINT
"The emergence of your toddler as a unique and separate individual is one of the primary developments of the second year."

Supporting Evidence

Attachment and Later Achievement

Alan Sroufe, Byron Egeland and their colleagues at the University of Minnesota's Institute of Child Development have been involved in the most comprehensive long-term study on the early attachments children form with their caregivers and how these attachments are related to later academic achievement. These researchers followed 174 children across a full 16-year span. They began measuring factors in the home environment, such as the attachment pattern between infant and parent, how autonomous the child was, how well the child could self-regulate, the overall home environment and overall maternal stress. They also took early measures of the children's IQ.

Next, the researchers tracked the performance of these children in school settings, measuring how well the children adapted to the school environment, as well as their scores on standardized tests in mathematics, reading recognition, reading comprehension, spelling and general information. What the researchers found was truly amazing. Early measures of IQ were clearly predictive of later academic achievement, but when IQ was equal, the factor most predictive of achievement was the strength and pattern of the parent-child attachment.

Speaking Their Minds

If you pay close attention to the words your toddler uses, you can virtually hear his sense of self develop. Around 18 months, a toddler has the ability to form mental pictures and create abstract ideas. He may, for example, rock his doll and pretend he's the mommy, or use a carrot as a drumstick. The ability to pretend means he has formed mental pictures and begun symbolic thought; these pictures and symbols help him put ideas together, which in turn, leads to more complex behaviors and emotions. All of these changes are reflected in his language about himself. Listen for the following developments and encourage his self-expression:

- **Labels Self and Others**

  Your toddler can now label himself and other people with appropriate personal pronouns, such as "me hot." Through his words, he is demonstrating further maturity of self.

- **Knows Self Has a Past**

  You toddler demonstrates having a "remembered" self – a self with a past (back as far as about to the end of the first year) that can be recalled through language. Eighteen- to 24-month-old children, for example, frequently imitate and reenact their own past actions.

Supporting Evidence

The Perfect Self-Image

One of the classic studies in a toddler's understanding of his self-image was conducted by Beulah Amsterdam at the University of North Carolina, Chapel Hill. Amsterdam placed a smidgen of rouge on the noses of a group of young children, then had the children sit in front of a mirror. The hypothesis was that if a child reached for the image of his nose in the mirror, he still had not formed a full sense of himself. If he looked at the mirror and then touched his own nose, however, he is thought to have distinguished himself from his reflection and seemed to recognize his true self. Touching his nose, in other words, is evidence that he has a sense of who he is and what he looks like.

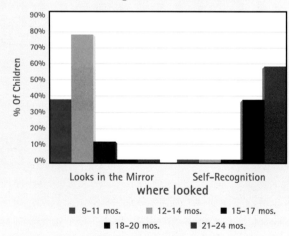

Self Recognition Increases Throughout the Second Year

Based upon data from Amsterdam, B.K. Mirror Self-Image Reactions Before Age Two. *Developmental Psychobiology 5* (1972), 297-305.

What's a Parent To Do?

A C T I V I T Y

Sit in front of a full-length mirror with your toddler standing in front of you. Point to your nose, and clearly and slowly say, "Nose." Point to his nose and do the same. Move across all the other elements of your face. As he gets better at this, make some mistakes, and let him correct you – he'll think it's hilarious.

B E N E F I T

Fosters language learning and builds self-awareness.

- **Starts to Internalize Do's and Don'ts**

  Your toddler can represent parental rules and evaluate the appropriateness of his behavior through language. When something goes wrong, the toddler might say, "Uh-oh," or "me fix." These phrases show a knowledge of social rules and a strong desire to follow these rules.

- **Increases Negative Verbalizations**

  Along with a broader vocabulary comes a broader range of negative verbalizations. By the end of the second year, most children have a few hundred words at their command. They can use this vocabulary to control their environment, telling you they have a "boo boo" and sending you for the bandage rather than just sitting down and wailing. They also use their words to express the whole range of their emotions, and to test adult reactions.

Parents Reduce Emotional Stress

Initially, your toddler views himself as someone who feels or experiences certain things, not as someone who is capable of doing anything to change what he feels or experiences. Until his awareness of himself as an agent of change kicks in – between 18- and 24-months – your toddler uses information in his environment to regulate his emotions. This realization is exemplified by the way toddlers check in with their parents when they are distressed. Although an 18-month-old will look to his mother for comfort when he finds himself in a distressing situation, it may take him several seconds to do so – several seconds of feeling very distraught. A 24-month-old toddler, however, has already developed a strategy for avoiding the distress: he'll look to his mother almost immediately for emotional comforting. It may not seem like such a big deal, but he has just demonstrated a thorough understanding that he has the power to understand his world and change his reaction to it.

> **KEY-POINT**
> "Growth in your toddler's intellectual and language skills provides the basics necessary for his emotional growth."

Be aware of the times when your toddler turns to you for help, and be sure to give him encouragement. Use body language, such as nodding your approval, and use lots of words that let him know he is OK: "You're OK," "You can do it," "Do you want me to hold you?" "Do you want to get down and try again?" "Good job!"

Meeting Adult Standards

As toddlers attain the ability to change the way they behave, parents come to have greater expectations for their toddlers as to what is appropriate and what is not appropriate behavior. There are rules which are set by the family, the community and society. One of your toddler's biggest jobs is to figure out these rules and to figure out that he has the ability to follow them. Before you expect too much, or too little of him, it's a good idea to know what your toddler is capable of during his second year of life.

- **Do I Know What They Want Me to Do?** Just as he learns to classify his blocks by size and his beads by color, your toddler will learn how to classify things or events as good and bad, right or wrong. A 14-month-old might look upon a dirty toy and think nothing of it, while a 19-month-old might call it "Yucky," and throw it on the ground. This is a recognition of the adult standard of keeping things neat and clean.

  Be consistent in how you apply rules – this will help your toddler understand that a rule is, in fact, a rule; it will also help when he decides to test the limits.

- **What Am I Supposed to Be Doing?** At 17 months, toddlers don't have a great understanding of goal-directed behavior – activities designed to lead to a specific outcome. It's not until around 20- to 24-months that toddlers are

What's a Parent To Do?

A C T I V I T Y

Act out one of your favorite stories.
Let your toddler be whichever character he chooses, and you be all the rest.
Use costumes and props as appropriate.

B E N E F I T

Teaches understanding of other people's motivations, intentions and inspires imaginative and imitative play.

able to work toward a major end result. Keep this in mind as you ask your toddler to complete a task, like building a tower out of blocks.

Toddlers love to do what they think adults consider good, so congratulate each small attempt he makes to complete a task.

- **How Does It Feel When I Do It?** Toddlers clearly relish it when they do something they know an adult will consider good, whether it's putting a scrap of paper in the garbage just like daddy, or pretending to water the plants just like mommy. You'll often see a toddler of this age clap in appreciation of his own efforts. This is also the age when the plea "me do" becomes a favorite refrain. Your toddler wants to please you and to take on new skills. Encourage his attempts and show him that you are, in fact, pleased.

- **How Does It Feel When I Can't Do It?** Just as he shows his happiness, your toddler also expresses his displeasure. Children in this age group get upset and frustrated when they can't accomplish what they're supposed to or that which they think you expect from them. For example, your toddler might do fine helping you mix the cake batter, but might accidentally splatter his shirt with chocolate. This can send him into a tailspin: he was doing everything just like mommy except for staying clean. Signs of distress might be fretting, slamming the spoon down or bursting into tears. Name your toddler's problem, validate it and help him find the solution: "I see you're frustrated and angry. Mommy gets frustrated sometimes, too. Can you help me put your shirt in the washing machine? Then we'll give you a clean shirt and finish baking the cake."

- **Deciding Whether Or Not to Do What Adults Consider Good Or Bad**

Although a 12- to 24-month-old is not at the prime age to test the standards the adults in his life have set (that behavior is reserved for next year!), he still may do it from time to time. Defiance is a logical way to test how firm the rules are and, as we mentioned above, a natural outgrowth of the developing self. It helps, during fits of defiance, to firmly restate the rules, such as, "We don't hit in this house," and to explain why; explanations are important for your toddler's long-term understanding of rules, and make them more likely to follow them: "It hurts people when we hit them; it's not nice to hurt people."

> **KEY-POINT**
> "Your emotional responses act as a model that helps your toddler respond with empathy."

Being Nice

One of the standards almost every parent sets for their toddlers is to be nice to others and to help them when

Supporting Evidence

Showing Concern for Others

Carolyn Zahn-Waxler and her colleagues at the National Institute of Mental Health have recently conducted research to examine whether toddlers look to comfort others when they are in distress. Zahn-Waxler followed 27 toddlers over the course of the second year to measure their ability to respond with empathy when someone else was in distress. Waxler found that some children just over a year old were able to respond empathetically, and even pro-socially — meaning he might try to comfort mom if she got hurt. By the close of the second year, 96 percent of the toddlers-all but one of the original 27 toddlers — responded empathetically, and both empathy and pro-social behavior increased starting around 18 to 21 months.

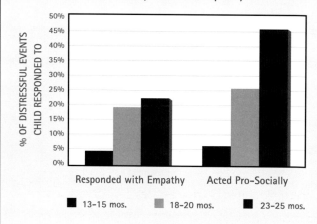

The Development of Empathy

Based upon data taken from Zahn-Waxler, C., Radke-Yarrow, M., Wagner, E., & Chapman, M. (1992). Development of concern for others. *Developmental Psychology, 28,* 126-136.

they are in distress. Psychologists call this "pro-social" behavior. Although humans have a natural propensity toward caring and empathy, it's the job of the parent to teach the specifics. Just like the rules about holding mommy's hand in the parking lot or picking up our toys, being nice is a social skill that has to be learned.

- **Parallel Play**

  In general, young toddlers are friendly and curious about each other. Although some children this age enjoy interactive play, most young toddlers don't really play with each other yet. They imitate actions and play side-by-side in what is known as "parallel play." Sharing is still a hard and distant concept at this point.

- **Empathy**

  Voluntary behavior intended to benefit another person, often termed pro-social behavior, can be observed around 16 months of age when children try to do something about someone else's grief or emotional experience. You'll find that between one-to two-years of age, your toddler develops a heightened empathetic concern for others in distress. At first he may react simply by crying or commenting. By the latter part of the second year, however, he translates this concern into action, *e.g.*, giving a stuffed animal to his friend who is crying. Through this behavior, your toddler is

gaining emotional insight into people and embarking on the path of caring for others.

- **Emotional Insight**

  Your toddler is experiencing an amazing period of growth as he gains emotional insights. He is recognizing his own emotions; remarking at the emotions in others; trying to coordinate his emotions, language, behavior and quest for independence, and attempting to meet social standards. This is no small feat! You can help simply by helping him recover from emotional upsets, supporting his efforts and applauding his growth.

Parents tell it like it is:

"I love the way our twins, Andrea and Ashley, take care of each other. If there's ever a bump or a bruise, there's also a loving hug or kiss, and a follow-up 'all better.'"
MICHAEL FRANCO,
FATHER OF ALICIA, ASHLEY AND ANDREA

Emotional Complexity

Near the end of the 12- to 24-month age range, your toddler's emotions become infinitely more complex. Until 18 months of age, toddlers have no basis for feeling emotions such as pride or guilt, because they can't think about their own behavior and other people's standards simultaneously. Once a toddler can recognize, think about and talk about himself in relation to other people, he'll begin to develop secondary emotions. These "self-conscious" emotions are more sophisticated because they are reflective and indirect. They do not appear until children are able to think about and evaluate themselves in terms of some social standard, rule or desired goal. Your toddler, for example, can be proud of his scribbling only after he judges his action to be admirable in the eyes of others. You say, "Nice writing, Andrew." He lights up, scribbles more and looks for your approval. Help your toddler understand these emotions by acknowledging them and reassuring him if they seem to overwhelm him:

- **Pride**

    Encourage all his efforts and reward him for his accomplishments with hugs and praise.

- **Shame:**

    Or failure to meet adult expectations – explain that what he feels is normal, and that you know he will learn better behavior as he grows.

- **Guilt**

    Praise him for knowing that he did something wrong. You can't feel guilt unless you know the rules.

"Our feelings are our most genuine paths to knowledge."
AUDRE LORDE, POET

What's a Parent To Do?

A C T I V I T Y
Draw a sad face on one (old) wooden spoon, and a happy face on another. Play act how each spoon must be feeling, then let him have a turn. Ask him which spoon matches how he's feeling today.

B E N E F I T
Gives him a way to communicate and understand his feelings.

Music's Impact on Development

Music's Impact on Development

What You'll Discover In This Section

"I would teach children music, physics and philosophy; but more importantly music, for in the patterns of music and all the arts are the keys to learning."

PLATO, GREEK PHILOSOPHER

- How music is rooted in the biology of our brains.

- How music and language are related.

- How music can foster develop- ment in areas as diverse as reading, mathematics and fine motor coordination.

- Why singing is so important to musical and intellectual development.

- How to create a musically enriched environment.

"Just as preschool children develop the foundation of their language-listening and speaking vocabularies long before they enter school, so must they develop the foundation for their music-listening and singing vocabularies before they enter school."

EDWIN GORDON, EARLY MUSIC EDUCATION SPECIALIST

Musical Growth and Delight

Music exerts a powerful force on the developing mind. For all the natural, simple delights it brings, we now have a growing body of evidence that early exposure and involvement with music can produce a number of positive effects. Several areas of the brain are affected by musical experiences, including areas that process memory and visual-spatial skills. Some researchers believe that musical experiences actually restructure thinking patterns, increasing the ways in which information is stored and processed. According to some studies, school-age children have an advantage when given music training; their mastery of core subjects such as math and reading improves. Though toddler-specific studies are less plentiful, experts in neuroscience, music and early childhood education have all concluded that music plays a

key role in creating an enriched learning environment for toddlers age 12 to 24 months.

Parents are sometimes led to believe that all they need to do to achieve the benefits of music is to play a little Mozart, but this far overstates the case. The research demonstrates that the benefits of music come as a result of getting your toddler actively involved with music. Listening to a wide variety of rich music, playing musical games, or letting your toddler experiment with high-quality musical instruments all play a positive role in her development. This kind of active involvement with music will not only foster your toddler's higher level intellectual development, but prepare her for a lifetime of musical enjoyment, as well.

Key Milestones in Musical Development

Age	Milestone
12 to 15 Months	• Increased Physical Response to Music — her physical reactions to music become more lively and last for longer periods of time. • Increased Control of Vocalization — she begins to vocalize more when she hears music and is better able to control her voice.
15 to 18 Months	• Becomes More Sensitive to Lower Frequencies — until this point, she hears higher pitch frequencies more clearly than lower pitches; at this point, her hearing range increases downward.
18 to 21 Months	• Matches Movements to Music — she is able to synchronize her movements to music for short periods of time. • Echoes Words — she begins to repeat parts of songs and join in when others sing. • Improved Pitch — she begins to develop better pitch.
21 to 24 Months	• Singing Longer Phrases — she begins to sing longer and longer songs, although her singing is still rhythmically simple. • Increase in Spontaneous Singing - she begins to spontaneously sing longer made-up songs, even in the absence of music. • Increase in Amount of Singing — she begins to sing more frequently throughout the day. • Increased Song Creativity — she begins to make up her own songs.

How Biology Connects Music to Emotions and Intelligence

Music is thought to have its roots deeply embedded in human history. Many scientists believe that music evolved as an early form of communication. Perhaps our ancestors used singing to warn each other of impending danger, to share a sense of joy or to broadcast their agony. With such valuable needs and uses for musical expression, music became biologically rooted in the brain. As humans evolved, specific structures in the brain became responsible for producing and processing musical information.

There are no areas in the brain, however, exclusively responsible for music, and many areas of the brain handle a variety of cognitive, emotional and musical tasks. Because these areas of the brain have multiple responsibilities, music, emotions and intelligence are inseparably linked:

- **Link to Intelligence**

  Studies of how the brain processes music demonstrate that many of the same areas responsible for the processing of music are also the same brain areas responsible for the processing of higher level intellectual functions, such as language, learning and memory. When the brain is stimulated by music, these areas are stimulated, as well.

- **Link to Emotions**

  Musical processing also shares many of the same areas used in the processing of emotions. For this reason, music can elicit some of our purest feelings. Because of this emotional connection, the pleasures of music are as accessible and as satisfying to a toddler as they are to the musically trained adult.

How Music Impacts the Developing Brain

There is now a great deal of evidence – listed below – that early exposure to music is likely to lead your toddler to many long-term benefits.

- Higher scores on tests of visual spatial reasoning – a skill required for many tasks, including mathematics.

- Increased brain response to musical tones – the amount of response was directly related to the age at which a musician began training. The earlier training began, the more response.

"...I believe that music training functions to organize a child's perceptions of space and time, just as numbers, language, color, shape and gestures organize a child's perception of musical sound."

JOYCE EASTLUND GROMKO,

EARLY MUSIC EDUCATION SPECIALIST

- Increased efficiency in the way the two hemispheres of the brain communicate. Musicians who began their training in childhood were shown to have a larger corpus callosum (a structure connecting the two hemispheres of the brain) than non-musicians.

- Improved reading scores – active engagement with music (such as singing) and early forms of music training can help toddlers fine-tune their ability to differentiate the sounds of language, which has been shown to be a necessary skill in both language and reading acquisition.

- Enhanced effects on gross and fine motor skills.

- Enhanced listening skills – children exposed to ample amounts of music were better able to concentrate for longer periods of time without interrupting the group.

Supporting Evidence

Linking Music and Math

Much of the research reported on the positive effects of music training has been related to visual-spatial abilities, which are abstract problem-solving skills critical to math understanding. Amy Graziano, Matthew Peterson and Gordon Shaw, at the University of California, Irvine, recently found a direct relationship between musical training and performance on mathematical tasks. They gave groups of second-graders either piano lessons, English lessons or no lessons. A proportion of each group of students also received added visual-spatial training by playing a specially designed video game. The students were then tested on their ability to perform math problems. Among the students who played the video game, the students who took piano lessons scored 26.7 percent higher than those who took English lessons, and 154.5 percent higher than those who took no lessons.

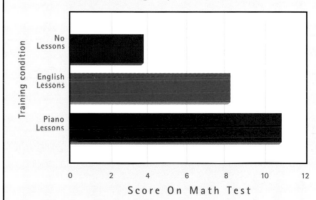

Music Training Improves Math Scores

Based upon data from Graziano, A.B., Peterson, M., and Shaw, G.L. (1999). Enhanced learning of proportional math through music training and spatial-temporal training. *Neurological Research, 21,* 139-152.

"Music is the manifestation of the human spirit, similar to language. Its greatest practitioners have conveyed to mankind things not possible to say in any other language."

ZOLTÁN KODÁLY, EARLY MUSIC EDUCATION PIONEER

- Enhanced tactile processing areas in the brain – musicians who began piano training prior to adolescence have larger sections of their brain dedicated to finger touch perception.

- Improved familiarity with musical forms – according to Cecilia Riddell, early musical education expert, early exposure to a wide variety of musical forms from a wide variety of cultures can enhance a love of music throughout a lifetime.

It is clear from these conclusions that music is a powerful force that your toddler should be encouraged to embrace. The goal is to give her a rich musical environment similar to the rich literary environment needed to learn how to speak, read and write.

The Language of Music

Language and music are parallel systems that develop in the same way and share many of the same attributes. In the first year of life, the precursors of early speech are impossible to distinguish from the precursors of spontaneous song. Toddlers come to understand music in the same way that they come to understand speech – by listening, following the non-verbal cues of their caretakers and opening their own mouths to practice making sounds.

What's a Parent To Do?

ACTIVITY

Draw faces on your own fingers. Make one look especially silly, and to the melody of "Are You Sleeping?" (also known as "Frere Jacques") sing the following rhyme. Start with your fingers closed, and as each new line is sung, let your toddler lift one of your fingers until she finds the silly face. At the end of the song, tickle her:

Where is big silly John?
Where is big silly John?
He's not here!
He's not here!
Where can he be hiding?
Where can he be hiding?
Here he is!

BENEFIT

Reinforces language development, self-awareness, fine motor skills and emotional identification.

- In speech, toddlers learn the names of objects when their parents point and name things. In music, toddlers learn the patterns of rhythm when their parents rock, sway and dance to the beat.

- In speech, toddlers learn the structure of sentences by listening for the sharp or drawn-out beginnings and ends of words. In music, toddlers learn the structure of music by listening for the sharp or drawn-out sounds of notes at the beginnings and ends of musical phrases.

- In speech, toddlers learn the meaning of words by listening to the different tones when they hear sounds such as "Stop!" and "I love you." In music, toddlers learn the meaning of melodies by listening to the tones in songs such as the "Old Gray Cat" or "Round and Round the Merry-Go-Round."

Supporting Evidence

Music and Language: Separate but Parallel

To examine the extent of the parallel between verbal language systems and musical systems, John M. Feierabend, T. Clark Saunders and colleagues at the University of Hartford looked at how pre-schoolers' memory for songs was affected by changes in the melody versus changes in the lyrics. The researchers presented a set of original songs to three- and five-year-olds, and then played them back in one of two ways: the original melody with new words or original words with a new melody. Feierabend and colleagues found that preschoolers' memory for the songs was impacted more by changes in melody than by changes in words, but that over time, the words and melody seem to become more intimately linked — that is, with repeated exposures to the song, the memory traces for melody and words ultimately become almost one and the same. These findings have led some researchers to hypothesize that one area in the brain (thought to be the left temporal lobe) is responsible for processing the melodic and lyrical components of a song while another area of the brain (thought to be the right temporal lobe) processes the lyrics.

"I think I should have no other mortal wants, if I could always have plenty of music. It seems to infuse strength into my limbs and ideas into my brain. Life seems to go on without effort, when I am filled with music."

GEORGE ELIOT, AUTHOR

Nurturing Musical Development

The Musicality of Common Games

There is a natural musical rhythm in the games that parents play with their toddlers. Anticipatory games such as peek-a-boo, hide-and-seek and tickling games all follow the same rhythmic pattern recognizable to professional musicians as a common way to grab, hold and sustain the excitement of an audience:

- Build the excitement for what is to come.
- Pause to increase anticipation.
- Let out all the stops for a climactic scene.
- Rest and relax to prepare to play again.

This pattern is almost universally recognized by people around the world, and many scientists believe the parallel between childhood games and musical structure is not a coincidence: these patterns are thought to be tapping into our earliest memories of human communication. Because there appears to be a natural understanding of this back and forth interactive pattern, this type of play is a great way to teach your toddler a number of skills, including sequencing and cause-and-effect relationships. While your toddler is playing a game which incorporates the elements listed above, she'll also be experiencing an almost musical

What's a Parent To Do?

ACTIVITY

Sit on the floor with your knees bent
and place your toddler on
your thighs, facing away from you.
As you recite the rhyme, bounce
your knee as if she is riding a horse:

Ride a cock-horse
to Banbury Cross
To see a kind lady,
up on a white horse
Rings on her fingers
and bells on her toes
She shall have music
wherever she goes

BENEFIT

Reinforces language development,
musical awareness and
gross motor skills.

build up of excitement for what is to come, pauses to increase anticipation, a climax and a restful period to regain energy for a repeat performance.

Sing a Song!

One of the most important ways of gaining musical understanding is through playing an instrument, and the most common and accessible instrument to play is our own voice. As we sing, we are directly involved in a complex process of coordination, involving the brain, the ears, the lungs, the diaphragm, the vocal chords, the lips and the teeth – but no one ever thinks about that when they sing. Humans tend to simply do it. Toddlers naturally bring song and music into their games, for example, and parents often use singing to communicate with their children. Throughout the world, parents speak to their young children in a much different way than they do with other adults or older children; with young children, parents

use a rhythmic and higher pitched sing-song voice known as "parentese."

As effective as parentese is at getting a child's attention, researchers have found that toddlers respond much more strongly when parents actually sing to them. The toddlers gaze intently and for much longer periods at a singing parent than they do at a speaking or gesturing parent. Singing provides children the cues and the repetition that helps them learn language skills. According to some experts in the field, singing may be one of the foremost ways to introduce babies to the sounds that comprise spoken language.

So sing! Sing about how much you love your toddler, about the flowers blooming in the garden and about putting on socks before putting on shoes. It's great fun to sing both familiar and made-up songs, and we can almost guarantee that your toddler will think you have the most amazing voice in the world. She may not jump right in and start singing with you just yet, but you will soon hear her singing short phrases from familiar songs, anticipating what comes next or moving to the beat of what you're singing. These are all signs that she is listening. When you think she's ready to jump in, sing very slowly and pause to let

Supporting Evidence

Musical Training Increases Test Performance

Is there any hard evidence that the types of musical training programs available for young children have any lasting impact on children's intellectual abilities? Joyce Eastlund Gromko and Allison Smith Poorman of Bowling Green State University have examined this issue by giving a group of three- and four-year-olds lessons in music and comparing their performance on spatial tasks against a group of children who did not receive this type of training. Gromko and Poorman designed their music training programs to parallel the types of early music programs that are now available to parents and their young children. This training included activities such as singing, clapping, ringing bells, playing hand chimes and playing triangles in synch to the music. After eight months of this type of music training, children were measured on their performance of visual-spatial reasoning – a skill noted for its relevance to mathematical understanding. The children who were in the training program scored seven percent higher on these mathematical tasks than did children who were not in a music training program.

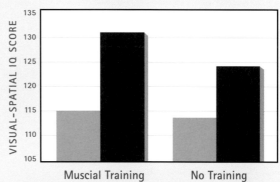

Early Music Training Aids Performance on Visual-Spatial Tasks

Based upon data from Gromko, J.E., and Poorman, A.S (1998). Effects of Music Training on Preschoolers' Spatial-Temporal Task Performance. *Journal of Research in Music Education, 46 (2) Summer*, pp. 173-181.

her fill in the blank. Sing "Twinkle, twinkle, little _____. How I wonder what you _____."

Music 101: The Toddler Course

Should you enroll your toddler in a specialized music program such as Music Together, KinderMusik, MusikGarten, or one of the many locally organized programs based on the Orf Schulwerk, Kodály, Suzuki or other methods? Clearly, we believe that it is fun, easy and effective to bring music into your toddler's life on your own; we also believe that you can enhance these positive effects even more by enrolling your toddler, and yourself, in a specialized early music program. These classes encourage listening, singing, movement and music-making in a group setting and bring a sense of routine to the enjoyment of music. If you do enroll in a program of this kind, look for the following elements:

"Toddlers are ready for music; their musical appetites are so big, they want to play those drums and triangles, and sing those songs and rhymes that they will soon sing themselves."

CECILIA RIDDELL, EARLY MUSIC EDUCATOR

What's a Parent To Do?

ACTIVITY

As you sing this song with your toddler, gently rub her hands together. At the word "Pop!" clap her hands together, then throw her arms wide open:

All around the carpenter's bench,
The monkey chased the weasel
The monkey thought it was all in fun
Pop! Goes the weasel

BENEFIT

Reinforces language development, musical awareness and gross motor skills.

- Developmentally appropriate instruments toddlers can handle on their own.

- Teachers trained in both music and early childhood education.

- Small class size – six to eight toddlers per instructor.

- Curriculum that stresses parental and even sibling involvement.

- Curriculum that involves both passive listening and physical engagement.

- A class that is fun for both you and your child.

"Music, the greatest good that mortals know and all of heaven we have here below."

JOSEPH ADDISON, AUTHOR

Creating an Enriched Musical Environment

Parents can encourage their toddler's musical, and intellectual, development by providing a variety of musical opportunities in an emotionally supportive and encouraging manner. It makes no difference whether or not you play an instrument or consider yourself musical. You don't need to be musical to sing, to dance, to clap to the beat or to listen to a great performance. You can create an enriched musical environment for your toddler by doing some or all of the following:

- **Sing Songs**

  You can sing many new songs to your toddler, whether she is being held, sitting in the car or lying down for a nap. Choose lots of songs with repeated words and phrases. Choose songs that are linked to activities so the child can participate even if she doesn't sing. Don't be afraid to sing songs that don't have words. Your toddler needs to be able to focus on short melodies and this gives her a chance to do it. Expect interest and attention, but not a singing response. She'll join in and sing when she's ready.

- **Interact With the Music**

  Do finger plays, action rhymes, tickling games and dances. Anything that helps you hear the music and play with its rhythms and patterns can be stimulating and fun.

- **Play Instruments**

  Keep high-quality musical instruments (such as triangles, finger symbols and recorders) in a special place and take them out at special times. Encourage your toddler to grasp musical instruments and make sounds with them in different ways. React with praise when she begins to handle instruments with care and sensitivity. Participate in her music-making, but don't dominate it.

- **Play Great Recorded Music**

  Play well-recorded music, with complex composition, in the background and foreground. Try a wide range of styles from a wide variety of sources. Without exposure to excellent music, your toddler will have no way to cultivate a preference for high quality music. Consider buying a child-friendly tape recorder (with easy-to-manipulate start and stop buttons and a volume lock) so she can occasionally be in control of the music herself.

- **Use Music to Set the Tone**

  One way to enjoy the immediate benefits of music is to use it to set the tone for a particular time of day. It often works when nothing else does. Quiet, calm music can help your toddler to go to sleep, get her to stop crying or calm her down before a big event. Rousing music can help get her going in the morning or motivate late-afternoon clean-up.

- **Improvise**

  Use music as the jumping off point for creative play. Create your own lyrics to familiar songs. Hum a song and see if your toddler can guess the song. Make up silly songs about things that happen during the day. Encourage your toddler to sing all kinds of songs – and tell her that her singing is music to your ears.

What's a Parent To Do?

ACTIVITY

Sit on the floor with your toddler and recite the following rhyme. Sometimes say the *"Quack! Quack! Quack"* loudly, other times say it softly. On the last verse, change the "did not come back" line to

"That little duck came running back!"
One little duck went out to play
Over the hill and far away
But the mommy duck said
Quack! Quack! Quack!
That little duck did not come back!

BENEFIT

Reinforces language development, musical awareness and voice control.

section seven

Monitoring Your Toddler's Development

Monitoring Your Toddler's Development

"You can observe a lot by just watching."

YOGI BERRA, BASEBALL GURU

What You'll Discover In This Section

- How early identification of developmental delays helps minimize long-term effects.

- How parents serve as a primary source of information on their toddler's development.

- What signs to look for.

"Where observation is concerned, chance favors only the prepared mind."
LOUIS PASTEUR, CHEMIST AND BIOLOGIST

The Power of Observation

One of the best ways to begin creating an enriched environment for your toddler is to observe him in an objective way. By closely watching the way he speaks and plays and interacts with other people, you can gain an increased awareness of the way his mind is working. This lets you follow his lead on favorite activities, introduce activities to develop areas that may need a boost and enjoy a deeper understanding of the way he interacts with his entire world. We have included a set of checkpoints to help you focus your observation and suggest a variety of ways you can use the information you discover.

> **KEY-POINT**
> **"Focus on overall development rather than any one area."**

Assessment in Its Place

The topic of early assessment is frequently debated in the field of early childhood development. Some experts argue that early assessment places too much emphasis on specific abilities and not enough emphasis on the big picture of development. These experts maintain that development happens in context and over time – not all at once, and maybe not on the day you decide to observe your child. Other experts focus more attention on the ability of a child to perform specific developmental tasks. The biggest concern of an ability-centered assessment is that a parent might place too much importance on specific tasks rather than on overall development. In an effort to get their child to progress or to perform, parents might stress learning how to draw a face rather than scribbling, or singing "Twinkle, twinkle little star" rather than "Twinkle, twinkle, I'm a car." Such short-sighted goals can be a danger to creativity, exploration and the development of problem-solving skills.

All-in-all, we believe that early assessment is an invaluable tool for understanding a toddler's development. The information gained through assessment can help parents become better at their job and can also ease any concerns they might have about their child's natural development. It can also help identify potential developmental delays at a point in which possible treatments can be most effective – we know that a toddler's brain is malleable, and because of this, the earlier a problem is detected, and the earlier intervention begins, the less likely the problem is to have a lasting impact.

When observations are made in context, over time, with the goal of increasing parental awareness, early assessment can yield very powerful insights into a toddler's overall development.

Angela Ballantyne, Ph.D., Pediatric Neuroscientist at the University of California, San Diego, and a specialist in the area of cognitive assessment, agrees. As Dr. Ballantyne says, "If a child is doing fine, assessment boosts everyone's ego/esteem, and can put some of the parent's apprehen-

sion to rest. If a child is having problems, then perhaps early intervention with a professional will be pursued – a situation that can have a meaningful impact on long-term outcomes."

The Benefits of Early Intervention

In the second year, there is a huge variability in development, which can make assessing normal behaviors difficult. One of the main reasons we recommend assessment is for early intervention. While early intervention is only applicable to a small number of children with delays in hearing, vision and certain types of cognitive processing, for these children, it is invaluable. By identifying areas of developmental delay, parents are in a much better position to understand the possible problem areas, put them into the context of overall development and seek help by appropriate professionals as necessary. The earlier these delays are found, the easier it is to develop appropriate and meaningful responses to them. Waiting until school age to address the delays is, according to Angela Ballantyne, "a gross disservice to the child, the parent and the schools."

KEY-POINT
"Early intervention is one of the biggest benefits of assessment."

Checkpoints

Even when considering individual differences in developmental timetables, it is a good idea for parents to monitor their child's development on a regular basis. Given how malleable a toddler's brain is early in life, the earlier a problem is identified and addressed, the less likely it is to have a lasting impact. To help you double-check your toddler's development, we've created a ***Checkpoint List*** within each age range. These lists cover some of the important basic developmental behaviors that most toddlers are engaging in by the end of each of the specific time periods.

These checkpoints were developed in conjunction with Andrea Ballantyne, an early childhood assessment expert at the University of California at San Diego, and amassed by culling through the literature on toddler behavior. Note that there is no Checkpoint list for the 18 through 20 month period because, with increasing age, the variability in the "normal range" of development increases, and it becomes very difficult to assign normative behavioral goals at three-month increments.

If you are not seeing the Checkpoint behaviors in your toddler during the appropriate age range, the first thing to do is check again; sometimes you just haven't caught her at the right time. If you still have concerns, you should, of course, contact your pediatrician for advice – and be persistent. Nobody knows your toddler as well as you do, and you should press for answers until you are comfortable with the response. Finally, we suggest that you consult some of the websites and books listed in our **Resource** section to gather additional information.

Parents tell it like it is:

"Mary and I had been practicing 'Head, Shoulders, Knees and Toes' for weeks before we went to grandma's, and we had it down pretty well. On the way there, all we did was talk about how fun it was going to be to sing our new song for everyone, but when we got there, only one of us was in the mood to sing – and it wasn't Mary. I spent the next two hours trying to convince my mother how great Mary was at 'Head, Shoulders, Knees and Toes.'"

BETH HOLDEN, MOTHER OF MARY ELIZABETH

Checkpoints – 12 Through 14 Months

By the end of this period, your toddler should demonstrate the following behaviors:

- **Startling**: demonstrates a moderate startle response to a loud noise.

- **Sitting:** sits without support.

- **Standing:** stands without support.

- **Responding to People:** responds selectively to different people.

- **Participating in Games:** participates in social games.

- **Grasping:** is able to grasp small objects.

- **Making Eye Contact:** makes eye contact with familiar people.

- **Imitating Gestures:** imitates the gestures of others.

- **Responding to Whispers:** responds to whispering.

Checkpoints – 15 Through 17 Months

By the end of this period, your toddler should demonstrate the following behaviors:

- **Recognizing Words:** recognizes words spoken to her.

- **Looking for Objects:** looks for hidden or covered objects.

- **Using Multiple Objects:** uses multiple toys when playing.

- **Demonstrating Affection:** demonstrates affection for primary caregivers or siblings.

- **Pointing at Objects:** shows interest in people or objects by pointing at them.

- **Producing Words:** produces even a single word.

- **Pretending:** engages in some level of pretend or imaginative play.

Checkpoints – 21 Through 24 Months

By the end of this period, your toddler should demonstrate the following behaviors:

- **Walking:** walks without assistance.

- **Grouping Objects:** groups objects by size, type or color.

- **Naming Objects:** uses words to name objects or people.

- **Knowing Body Parts:** knows, or points to, body parts.

- **Imitating:** shows interest in imitating the behavior of others.

- **Demonstrating Pride:** shows a sense of pride in accomplishment, *e.g.*, laughing or smiling when completing a game or puzzle.

- **Responding to Language:** responds when spoken to.

- **Engaging Others:** engages others in play, through either gestures or words.

- **Turning Pages:** shows interest in turning the pages of a book.

- **Pointing at Pictures:** shows interest in pointing to, or naming, the pictures in a book.

- **Solving Problems:** attempts to solve problems, such as climbing on the bed to retrieve a toy.

"The best assessments take place over a period of time rather than in the space of a single day."

STANLEY GREENSPAN, CLINICAL CHILD PSYCHIATRIST

section eight

Ages and
Stages

12 through
14 Months

Ages and Stages

12 through 14 Months

What You'll Discover | In This Section

"...the wiring diagram organization of the brain is embellished really rather dramatically, I mean 20 percent is a big change if you think about it, as a function of experience."

WILLIAM T. GREENOUGH, NEUROBIOLOGIST

- Ages and Stages Activity Guide.
- What's Happening: 12 through 14 Months.
- Activities to Nurture Intellectual Development.
- Activities to Encourage Language Development.
- Activities to Nurture a Love of Music.
- Activities for Psycho-Motor Development.
- Activities for Social-Emotional Development.
- Books to Add to Your Library.

Five Guiding Principles

1. Each of these activities had to be great for your toddler's developing mind.

2. Each had to be one that you would enjoy doing and that could easily become part of your life.

3. Each had to be appropriate for the developmental capabilities of toddlers in this age range.

4. Each had to be safe.

5. The completed list had to include activities ranging from tried-and-true basics to new and unique ideas.

I t's easy to share enriching experiences with your toddler because toddlers are so thrilled by it all. They adore it when you pretend you're a horse, crack up when you tickle their tummies and love it when you give them something to squish or mash. These are activities that come naturally to many families with 12- to 24-month-olds. After reading through the sections at the start of this guidebook, however, you may be wondering what else you could be doing to nourish your toddler's developing mind.

To help you bridge the gap from information to action, we asked our team of experts in child development, early childhood education and neuroscience to come up with a list of enriching activities to do with toddlers during their second year of life. In putting this list together, we used five guiding principles.

Ages and Stages

The sections in our book are all organized by topic (music, language, etc.) to give you a comprehensive understanding of key areas impacting cognitive development – but because the things you can do with a 12-month-old are so different from the things you can do with a 24-month-old, the activities in this section are organized by age: 12 through 14 months; 15 through 17 months; 18 through 20 months; and 21 through 24 months.

We start each **Ages and Stages** section with an overview of the major developments that occur during this time and the important activities that go along with them. This is just to remind you of the big picture before you delve into the details of what's fun and enriching to do. As you read through these events and ideas, remember that toddlers develop according to their own schedules. There is a very wide variation of development in the second year of life, and as a result, a very wide range of schedules. Our timelines and charts should be seen as general guidelines to the big picture of toddler development. We may discuss walking in the 12 to 14-month range, for example, but it's perfectly normal for your toddler to take her first step at 16 months.

What's Happening?

Following the introduction of each **Ages and Stages** section, you'll find a milestone chart entitled, "What's Happening?" This chart includes the major developmental domains: perception and cognition; vocalizations and language; social-emotional; and motor skills. This chart gives you the opportunity to see, at a glance, how your toddler's skills and faculties are growing. Again, these charts are designed as general guidelines. Your toddler may develop according to her own unique style, which is just as it should be. If you have any concerns about your toddler's development, see the Checkpoint boxes in the **Assessment** section on page 89.

Your Child's Library

Each **Ages and Stages** age range includes a recommendation of great books to read aloud to your toddler. The idea is to help you build a fun, useful and long-lasting library. Start with some of the books listed for the 12 through 14 month period, then add a few listed for 15 through 17 months, and so on. All the books on the list are either award-winners (Newbury winners for writing, Caldecott winners for illustration, or Globe-Horn, Young Reader's Choice, Giverny or Golden Kite awards for overall excellence) or they're books that have received high praise from our panel of parent reviewers or our board of advisors. These books are sure to hold your toddler's interest for many years to come.

Finding Inspiration

We've named each activity on our list, explained it and described the benefit it will bring to your toddler. We suggest you read through them all, even the ones that are not specifically for your toddler's age. There are so many good ideas, you'll find inspiration in every age range. Keep in mind that you don't have to stop an activity your toddler enjoys just because the time period has ended. Creating variations and expanding these activities can provide you and your toddler with ideas for many years to come. No matter when you choose to share these activities with your toddler, do so with some level of moderation; while enriching his environment is a good thing, over-stimulation is not. Your toddler will provide you with great cues, such as walking away or throwing a block down in frustration, when he's had enough.

Playing It Safe

As with everything you do with your toddler, safety should be the top priority. We make a lot of suggestions for things to do in the bath and the highchair, and you would never want to leave a toddler alone while you dash to get one of the things you need to play the game. You would never give a toddler something to play with that's smaller than his fist (unless you intend for him to eat it) and although we do suggest some games that involve string or tying things together, we intend that these be done under constant supervision. Toddlers are curious and sometimes fearless little creatures; they can easily get into more trouble than they can handle. Let them explore, but make sure you're there to perform a quick rescue when needed.

At the start of the second year, right at the time when most toddlers are standing up to walk, they experience several major cognitive and perceptual developments. Their capacity for remembering people, actions and objects increases, as well as their understanding of how an action can cause an outcome. They also begin to figure out how to create a mental representation of the world. As a result of these advances, toddlers of this age love games that involve their memory, such as hide-and-seek, peek-a-boo and lift-the-flap books that feature simple objects.

Exploration occupies a huge part of a young toddler's time. You'll see him spending extended periods of time staring at objects, checking out the details of their physical qualities and trying to find a deeper understanding of how things work. This is a perfect time to provide pop-up toys that let him explore and produce an action. Good choices are boxes with dials, switches and buttons that cause characters to appear. Try to avoid pop-ups that are too loud or too complex; even a jack-in-the-box can be too frustrating at this age because the crank is too hard to turn.

Frustration in general may become more frequent during this time period. Your toddler is just beginning to understand that he is capable of doing things and as a result he wants to try everything–including things that are still beyond his abilities. The result is often frustration. Be patient, supportive and lend a helping hand whenever he needs it.

As a result of all his watching and his increased intellectual capacities, your toddler will engage in more and more imitative play. He'll want to practice doing what he sees you doing. Give him a wooden spoon and a plastic bowl for cooking, a small broom for sweeping and a little trowel for digging in the garden. Praise his efforts to help around the house.

In addition to exploration and imitation, toddlers at this age enjoy placing objects into distinct (though by no means perfect) categories. To help foster these skills (which are precursors to full-fledged math skills), introduce games and toys that encourage categorization, e.g., placing all of the yellow rings in one pile, and all the blue rings in the other. He'll love helping you pick all the socks out of the laundry pile or finding the biggest cantaloupe in the bin at the grocery store.

In the area of language development, your toddler's comprehension is growing at a rapid rate. Talk to him as much as you can, using as many words as you can in as many settings as you can. Read to him frequently, and consider foreign language toys, games or radio stations to expose him to a wide variety of linguistic sounds. Although your toddler can't use words to tell you everything he is thinking, the words he can say, along with his expressions and gestures can be used as reliable cues to what he's trying to say. Let him know you understand. To give him a chance to show he understands what you're saying, try asking him to follow a short set of directions, such as placing the dirty clothes in the hamper or picking up a book and putting it in the bookcase. Praise him for his efforts.

Along with a growing sense of independence come emotional reactions that can often be frightening for your toddler. Being independent can be scary, and these feelings can produce ambivalence. "I want to do it myself," your toddler may think, "but I also need your help;" "I want to explore that other room... but I'm scared to go by myself." This ambivalence is often characterized by what many developmental psychologists refer to as negativism. Twelve months is still the early stages of negativism, but it's not too soon to start finding ways of encouraging independence while offering reassurance.

"When we speak to our children, we provide them with a kind of mental exercise...the experience we give them, the mental exercise we provide, causes their brains to change."

PATRICIA KUHL, NEUROSCIENTIST

WHAT'S HAPPENING: 12 THROUGH 14 MONTHS

Perception & Cognition	Vocalizations & Language	Social-Emotional	Motor
• Points to 'ask' for things he wants.	• Understands short commands from parents and caregivers.	• Focuses on a person who is speaking to him.	• Uses his thumb and an additional finger to lift objects.
• Begins to understand the concept of books, *e.g.*, loves to turn the pages.	• Applies labels to whole groups of objects, *e.g.*, "dah" might be a word for dog, cat, horse or any other four-legged animal.	• Increased focus on primary caregivers, often with signs of affection, such as hugs and kisses.	• Is able to drink from a cup with a lid.
• May observe a single object for extended periods of time.		• Begins to become more assertive.	• Is able to wave hello and goodbye.
• Explores many objects with his mouth.	• Word production increases — although still low — but pronunciation is still not clear.		• Is able to stand without support for a few seconds, and may be taking a few steps.
• Deliberately introduces variations into the games he is playing — such as peeking at you over the top of the chair rather than over the side.	• Often uses gestures as a form of sign language to communicate.		• Begins to climb on a variety of objects, such as chairs and couches.
• Remembers tastes, smells and textures of things.			

ACTIVITIES FOR BABIES FROM 12 THROUGH 14 MONTHS
ACTIVITIES TO NURTURE INTELLECTUAL DEVELOPMENT

Activity	Description of the Activity	Benefit
The Hat Trick	Take an old hat (preferably, one that is deep enough to hide objects dropped into it, but shallow enough for your toddler to reach the bottom), and take turns dropping in blocks. You can count them as they go in, name their color or drop them in a special order.	Exercises fine motor skills, strengthens memory skills and teaches numbers and language concepts.
Walking on Water	Find a small wading pool, take off your shoes and go for a walk across the water. Hold your toddler's hands as you go. Point out how much harder it is to lift your feet and take a step in water than it is to do it on solid ground.	Develops awareness of muscles, senses and cause-and-effect relationships.
Feed the Birds	Place a bird feeder outside your child's window. You can make a good one by putting peanut butter on a pinecone and rolling it in sesame seeds.	Provides a personal experience of nature and wild animals, and inspires imaginative play.
Read and Smell	Create your own book of smells. Staple together three or four sheets of paper. Drip vanilla on one page, glue a eucalyptus leaf to another and spray perfume on the last.	Builds pre-literacy skills, inspires imaginative play and provides a unique tactile experience.
The Big Brush Up	In a medium size box, place a hairbrush, a toothbrush and a scrub brush — and let your toddler explore.	Provides a great tactile experience and strengthens memory skills.
The Crawling Box	Turn a large box over on its side. Fill it up with lots of soft stuffed animals and show your toddler how to crawl in. Next time, fill the box with tennis balls and then try warm sheets just out of the dryer.	Provides a great tactile experience.
A Walk in the Park	Find a freshly mown lawn, take your toddler's shoes off and let the grass tickle his toes! Talk about how different it is to walk on grass than it is to walk on the rug or the floor.	Provides a great tactile experience and inspires imaginative play.
Card Shark	Use a full deck of regular playing cards. Show your toddler how to sort them into piles of clubs and hearts, and later, red and black.	A perfect lesson in color and shape concepts.

Activity	Description of the Activity	Benefit
Styrofoam Gingerbread People	Use cookie cutters to trace characters on a thin piece of Styrofoam. Cut out and decorate the characters, using pens, scraps of felt or fake fur. Use the characters to stage a dance, a play or a tea party.	Exercises fine motor skills and inspires imaginative play.
Wet n' Wild Rocks	Go out to the garden, and bring in rocks of different sizes, shapes and textures. Wash the rocks in the sink, and have your toddler watch how the color and textures change when they are wet.	A great example of cause-and-effect relationships that also teaches color, size and shape concepts.
Gone Fishing	Tie string to a favorite toy and then wrap the string through chairs and around furniture. Walk with your toddler as you create the maze, then let him pull the toy back in, just as if he were landing a fish. Monitor closely and properly dispose of string when you are finished.	A great example of cause-and-effect relationships that also develops gross motor skills.
Body Paint	Finger paints are not just for fingers anymore! Try dipping his foot or his elbow in the paint and show him how to paint with these body parts — you can even do this with pudding! Make a growth chart of finger painted handprints or footprints.	Teaches cause-and-effect relationships, provides a unique tactile experience and provides a concrete example of growth.
Match Maker	Choose a favorite toy, such as a stuffed animal or a car, and go on a hunt to find things that are the same color, the same size or the same texture as the toy. Collect the similar things in a small box, if you can.	Inspires imaginative play and encourages an understanding of pre-math and categorization skills.
Measuring Cup Castles	Take some measuring cups out to the sandbox. Fill up both the 1/4 cup scoop and the full cup scoop with sand; have your toddler hold one in each hand, and tell him which one weighs more. Now pour them out in to separate piles, and tell him which cup held more sand. For a variation, try wetting the sand.	Demonstrates cause-and-effect relationships, teaches pre-math skills and develops fine motor skills.

Activity	Description of the Activity	Benefit
My Nose Knows	Sit in front of a full-length mirror with your toddler standing in front of you. Point to your nose, and clearly and slowly say, "Nose." Point to his nose and do the same. Move across all the other elements of your face. As he gets better at this, make some mistakes, and let him correct you — he'll think it's hilarious.	Fosters language learning and builds self-awareness.
One Book, Two Book, Red Book, Blue Book	Sit on the floor in front of a bookcase with your toddler in your lap. Looking at the shelves, slowly count the books. Start with just a few books, then gradually increase the number. Try sorting books by colors, too.	Builds pre-literacy, counting and number skills.
Rock Plop	Fill a pail or a bowl with a few inches of water. Hold a small rock about six inches above the water, and let it drop. Try another one about a foot or so above the water. Help your toddler try this, then move to a slightly larger rock. Be careful not to use any rocks that would hurt if they landed on a toe.	Demonstrates cause-and-effect relationships, and develops fine motor and pre-math skills.
Through the Looking Glass	Take turns looking in a hand-held mirror. Cover the mirror with colored cellophane, and try it again. Try combining yellow and green cellophane, blue and red, etc.	A good example of cause-and-effect relationships that also teaches color concepts and expands self-awareness.
The Tape Test	Stick a piece of tape on your baby's clothes, and let him have fun peeling it off. Let him take a turn at putting it on you.	Strengthens fine motor skills and also teaches a lesson in cause-and-effect relationships.
Socks Here, Shirts There	On the outside of your child's dresser, place a picture of the various items that go in the drawers. Label each picture with a word that describes the item. When it's time to get out socks (or underwear or a shirt), ask him to find where the socks are.	Builds pre-literacy skills and encourages both memory and independence.
Stacks and Nests	Save the containers from plastic fruit cups or yogurt. Make sure there are no sharp edges. Clean them out and use them as nesting cups. Stack them, hide toys inside them, hide toys under them, etc.	Strengthens fine motor, counting and memory skills.

Activity	Description of the Activity	Benefit
Teddy in the Cave	This is a tried-and-true way to engage your toddler in peek-a-boo. Start by playing a make-believe game with your baby's favorite stuffed animal. Have the animal go for a walk under a blanket. If he doesn't search for the teddy on his own, ask him to get it for you as part of the game.	Exercises memory skills, inspires imaginative play and encourages social skills.
Texture Rings	Tie small strands of fabric (short enough not to pose a strangulation risk) into interwoven circles. Make sure one ring is silky, one coarse, one soft, etc.	Provides a great tactile and visual experience, inspires imaginative play and teaches size and shape concepts.
Paper Bag Lab	Help your toddler crumple newspaper and stuff it into paper bags — be sure to use paper and not plastic. Tape the bags shut, and become a scientist, testing to see what sound the bag makes if you squeeze it this way, what shape you can form if you squish it that way. Try the same with wax paper or aluminum foil, and see how things change.	Demonstrates cause-and-effect relationships and also teaches shapes and sound concepts.
What's on the Line?	Use brightly colored yarn to tie toys to your toddler's highchair. Let them dangle off the tray. Encourage your child to pull them up to see what can be found at the end of the line. As he gets older, ask him what toy he's pulling up before he can even see it. Monitor carefully and properly dispose of yarn when finished.	A good example of cause-and-effect relationships that also develops memory.
Touch and Feel Book	Make your own texture book by stapling together pages of varying roughness. One page might be a very fine grain of sandpaper, the next a piece of silk, the next a piece of burlap and the final page of piece of plastic.	Builds pre-literacy skills, develops fine motor skills and provides exposure to a variety of textures.
Wake Up, Nose	Create a ritual around wake-up time, by *waking up* the different parts of your child's body. Start by touching the nose and saying, "Wake up, nose!" Move onto the ears, elbows, ankles and so on.	Builds self-awareness and encourages social skills.

Activity	Description of the Activity	Benefit
Water Bags	Fill and seal two zipper bags with water. Place one in the freezer for about an hour. When it's nice and cold, place the second bag in the microwave for a few seconds. (You can also simply fill the second bag with lukewarm water from the tap.) Let your toddler hold and squish each bag. Describe the differences in temperature, and how both bags contain the same thing.	Demonstrates cause-and-effect relationships, provides a unique sensory experience and teaches about both temperature and the physical properties of water.
What's in the Washcloth?	As part of your bathtime ritual, wrap some of your child's favorite bath toys in washcloths. Line them up beside the bath or sink, and let him discover what's inside. Throw in the occasional surprise, such as his shampoo bottle or a tube of toothpaste.	A ritual that develops memory skills and encourages social skills.

ACTIVITIES TO ENCOURAGE LANGUAGE DEVELOPMENT

Activity	Description of the Activity	Benefit
A Few of My Favorite Things	Slip pictures of some of your child's favorite things into the plastic insert sheets of a three-ring binder. Let him choose some of the pictures out of catalogs and magazines. Rotate them often. You can read this book together, naming each item. He can also sit by himself and flip through the pictures.	Builds pre-literacy skills and vocabulary, and inspires imaginative play.
Name that Bird	Sounds are everywhere! Take a seat on the front lawn or a park bench and name every sound you hear — the dog barking, the car honking, the sound of your neighbor mowing the grass, the birds singing, etc.	Encourages social skills, builds sound awareness and gives meaning to everyday events.
Raindrops Keep Falling on My Head	While giving your child a bath, gently shower him with drops of water from a washcloth or from your fingers. Sing the "Raindrops" song as the water falls.	Provides a unique tactile and musical experience, builds language skills and encourages social skills.
Story Time for Parents	Pull your toddler into your lap, and instead of reading him a children's book, read him what *you* want to read — the newspaper, a magazine, a recipe, a letter from a friend, etc.	Builds pre-literacy skills and encourages social skills.

Activity	Description of the Activity	Benefit
Cha Cha Cha	Add beans to a can or container with a lid, about one-third full. Play and/or sing some of your toddler's favorite songs, but at the end of each verses, add a "Cha Cha Cha" and shake the can of beans.	Develops musical awareness and fine motor skills.
Here's a Little Bug	Sit on the floor with your toddler between your legs. Recite the following rhyme as you run your fingers along the body part you're describing: *Here's a little bug, crawling up your leg* *Crawling up your leg,* *Crawling up you leg,* *Here's a little bug, crawling up you leg* *He's gonna get your tummy (or toes, or ears ...)*	Reinforces language development, musical awareness and self-awareness.
Jack and Jill	Recite the nursery rhyme, "Jack and Jill" and encourage your toddler to join in. At *"up the hill,"* playfully raise your voice, and draw out the words. Do the reverse at *"fell down."* Finally, add some "Doo-wops," adding playfulness by taking your voice down as you finish: *Jack and Jill went up the hill* *To fetch a pail of water* *Jack fell down, and broke his crown* *And Jill came tumbling after.* *Doo-wop! Doo-wop! Doo-wop!*	Reinforces language development, musical awareness and social skills.
Jack Had a Kitty	Recite the following rhyme. Clap your hands on the major beats at the start and the end of each line: *Jack had a kitty* *Jack had a cat* *Jack put kit-cats* *In his hat*	Reinforces language development, musical awareness and fine motor skills.

Activity	Description of the Activity	Benefit
Rum Puddle	Sit on the floor and give your child a small drum or a can with a lid on it. Recite the following rhyme and encourage your toddler to keep the beat on his drum: *Pick a little blue bird* *Pick a little star* *Rum puddle, rum puddle, biff, boom bam!* *Give it to Peter* *Give it to Pam* *Rum puddle, rum puddle, biff, boom bam!* *Point to the east* *Point to the west* *Rum puddle, rum puddle, you're the best!*	Reinforces language development, musical awareness and fine motor skills.
The Wind Blows High	Recite the following rhyme. Lower your voice as you say *"low;"* raise it as you say *"high."* We think you know what to do when you get to the tickle part: *The wind blows low,* *The wind blows high,* *It tickled my nose as it went by!* *Tickle, tickle, tickle!*	Reinforces language development, musical awareness and social skills.
This Little Pig Danced a Merry Jig	Sit on the floor with your toddler facing you. Take off his socks and shoes then sing this merry little jig. Take each toe in your hand as you name it in the rhyme: *This little pig danced a merry, merry jig* *This little pig ate candy* *This little pig wore a blue and yellow wig* *This little pig was a dandy,* *But this little pig never grew to be big* *So they call him tiny little Andy*	Reinforces language development, musical awareness, self-awareness and social skills.

Activities for Babies from 12 through 14 Months
Activities for Psycho-Motor Development

Activity	Description of the Activity	Benefit
Bowling, Part II	Make bowling pins out of empty soda cans by covering the sharp opening with plastic covers. Show your toddler how to use a foam ball to scatter the pins. As he gets better and better, move him farther and farther from the cans.	Develops both fine and gross motor skills and demonstrates cause-and-effect relationships.
Climbing the Stairs	Help your toddler practice going up and down the stairs. Many toddlers can handle going up before they can master coming down, so spend a good deal of time helping him learn how to crawl down the stairs backward. Monitor closely for safety.	Exercises gross motor skills and encourages social skills.
Pokey Holes	Cut out three holes from the top of a diaper wipes box. Make sure the holes are a little larger than the size of your fingers. Close the box, and poke your finger through each of the holes. Encourage your toddler to take a turn.	Develops fine motor skills and self-awareness.
Tetherball for Tots	Attach a piece of string to a light beach ball using duct tape. Hang the ball from the ceiling at a height that he can easily reach, and show him how to hit it. As he masters this, and as he grows, elevate the ball. Monitor closely, and properly dispose of string when you are finished.	Strengthens both fine and gross motor skills and demonstrates cause-and-effect relationships.
Push Button	Let your child have an old calculator, preferably one with large buttons. Show him what happens when he pushes the buttons. Encourage him how to use the calculator as a cash register when he's playing grocery store.	Builds fine motor skills, inspires imaginative play and provides a lesson in cause-and-effect relationships.
The Two-Person Clap	Place one small ball or block in your toddler's hands and another in yours. Practice knocking the balls or blocks together.	Demonstrates cause-and-effect relationships, develops fine motor skills and provides practice in coordinating more than one item at a time.

Activity	Description of the Activity	Benefit
A Book of Me	Using a three-ring binder, plastic insert sleeves and pictures of your toddler, make a book in which he's the star.	Builds pre-literacy skills, develops self-awareness and provides practice with symbols.
Family Tree	Before a family or friend get-together, make a family tree that has the picture of every family member or friend who will be attending.	Strengthens memory, encourages social skills and eases stranger anxiety.
Matching Boo Boos	On those sad occasions when your toddler is in need of a bandage, try placing one on one of his favorite stuffed animals as well.	Helps emotional regulation and inspires imaginative play.
That's My Shirt	As your toddler outgrows some of his infant clothes, use them to dress up some of his stuffed animals.	Encourages social skills and inspires imaginative play.
The Bear and the Barrier	Place a small barrier, such as a couch pillow, between you and your toddler. Sing "The Bear Went Over the Mountain" and encourage your child to cross the barrier and come to you.	Reinforces language development, musical awareness and problem-solving skills.
Wind, Rain and Snow	When bad weather comes, get out and experience it! Bundle up your toddler, then step outside to let the wind whip through your hair, feel the raindrops on your tongue and let the snow alight on your fingers. Use the moment to teach new vocabulary and talk about what's happening around you.	Strengthens vocabulary and provides a unique tactile experience.

"A baby's brain is not simply a miniature of the adult's. It is a dynamically changing structure that records its experience in its wiring."

CARLA SHATZ, NEUROBIOLOGIST

Books to Add to Your 12- through 14-Month-Old's Library

100 First Words *By Edwina Riddell*
There are lots of nice first word books on the shelves of the bookstores, and this is certainly one of them. One of the things we particularly like about this book is that it depicts babies and toddlers engaged in everyday activities. This is what makes it easy for your toddler to relate to the actions and the words that are associated with them.

ABC: The Anne Geddes Collection *By Anne Geddes*
It's a toss-up whether adults or toddlers love this book more. Anne Geddes brings together a whole alphabet of whimsical, entertaining and engaging examples of her signature image – babies. Each baby is dressed in a costume or perched on a prop representing a letter of the alphabet – such as a bee or a duck.

Baby's World: A First Picture Catalog *By Stephen Shott and Monfried Lucia (illustrations)*
Babies love to look at other babies and that is exactly what they get to do in this lovely collection of brightly colored photographs. The book is a hefty 40 pages, but the photographs are neatly categorized into sections, so it's easy to find the toy section or the color section.

Big *By Keith Haring*
Big clothes. Big colors. Big (sized) words. This is a book that toddlers will latch onto for its sheer cuteness. It introduces colors by showing different people wearing different pieces of big, colorful clothing.

Children Just Like Me *By Barnabas and Anabel Kindersley, and Dorling Kindersley (photography)*
Filled with photographs of children from around this world, this pictorial exposé introduces children to the cultures, families, schools and games of the world. A warm and educational book.

Color Farm *By Lois Ehlert*
The bright colors and textures of this Caldecott-winning book let toddlers use shapes to make their own menagerie of farm animals. On each page, you'll discover a new shape, which can be punched out of the book and combined with other shapes to make a rooster, a pig, a cow, etc.

Elmer's Colors *By David McKee*
Elmer is a patchwork quilt elephant and one of our favorite characters for young children. In this book, Elmer introduces children to colors by talking about his own unique hues. Other McKee works, such as "Elmer," "Elmer's Friends" and "Elmer in the Snow" are all great choices, too.

Five Little Monkeys Jumping on the Bed *By Eileen Christelow*
Reading this book is contagious – so much so that we can almost guarantee you'll never get the rhyme out of your head. The action starts as mama puts her five adorable little monkeys to bed. The problem is, the babies are not quite ready to go to sleep, and as soon as mama is gone, they start to jump on the bed. Mama calls the doctor, of course, and we all know what the doctor says but still the monkeys keep jumping.

Friends in the Park *By Simms Taback*
A wonderful book of photos celebrating the ethnic and physical diversity of a group of children playing in the park. This is a very nice introduction to the many ways in which people are different and a celebration of the many ways in which we are the same.

Good Times With Teddy Bear *By Jacqueline McQuade*
What could be more comforting than following a teddy bear as he makes his way through his day? This story has a simple theme, large letters describing the activity at hand and an area where important elements from the picture are highlighted – all of which add up to a touching, engaging and useful book.

Have You Seen My Duckling? *By Nancy Tafuri*
This picture story makes for a nice parable for you and your child as he begins to explore his world. The mama duck is searching for her baby, but the baby duck is off having adventures only careful readers can see. Toddlers never tire of finding the duckling and in the end, the mama duck finds her, too.

Mama, Do You Love Me? *By Barbara Joosse and Barbara Lavallee (illustrations)*
This book has a common theme – a parent expressing to a child how much the child is loved. What sets this story apart is that it takes place in the Alaskan wilderness and the child is a little Inuit girl. The story alone is lovely, and the deep and calming muted tones of the artwork are delightful.

On the Day I Was Born *By Deborah Chocolate and Melodye Rosales (illustrations)*
This book is a pure celebration of life for people of all backgrounds. It follows an African-American family as they greet the arrival of a new baby into the household. The pages take us

through a journey of welcome, with symbols and illustrations that highlight and celebrate the event in grand style.

Owly *By Mike Thaler and David Wiesner (illustrations)*
Every toddler needs to hear how much he's loved, and this story sends the message loud and clear. It's told in the simplest of terms, with illustrations produced by a Caldecott–winning artist. Even the most stoic parents cannot help being moved by this story.

Play Rhymes *By Marc Brown*
Don't know what to do during that lull in the middle of the day? These 12 familiar rhymes are paired with activities that are fun and engaging. The combination is great for entertainment and good for building language skills.

Ready for Red: *My First Colors By Candace Whitman*
This book is made up of a series of short and lovely rhymes, all with cross-cultural overtones, all focused on the color red. The montage of watercolor paper backgrounds is gorgeous and the pictures are captivating.

Spot's Favorite Colors *By Eric Hill*
This is one in the famous series of Spot books. It is a wonderful introduction to a wonderful character, who is experiencing the full range of colors in his world. Spot sees everything from a white snowman to a red bike to a pink birthday cake. The chunky board book packaging of this story makes it especially easy for even little children to hold onto.

Spring is Here *By Tao Gomi*
Publishers Weekly calls this "the perfect picture book." The simple story of the seasons features a newborn calf that grows as the seasons change throughout the year. Gomi has set his tale against a striking pink background that is sure to catch your attention and hold your toddler's interest.

Ten Little Dinosaurs *By Pattie Schnetzler and Jim Harris (illustrations)*
This book has everything to recommend it. Let's start with the 3-D bugged-out eyes on the cover: they are jiggly and fun, and toddlers can't resist them. Next, there are the dinosaurs themselves. The 10 little dinosaurs they will meet in this story are some of the most loveable. Third is the catchy rhyme (reminiscent of "Ten Little Monkeys") that will make the introduction of dinosaur words a piece of cake.

Ten, Nine, Eight *By Molly Bang*
A little girl's room is a magical place, especially when dad is there and it's time to get ready for bed. This story makes for a soothing bedtime ritual as father and daughter count down to sleep.

There Was an Old Lady Who Swallowed a Fly *By Simms Taback*
Take a funny folk song, add ridiculous side comments, silly cutouts and fabulous artwork and what do you have? A great retelling of an American classic.

This is the Way We Eat Our Lunch: A Book About Children Around the World *By Edith Baer and Steve Bjorkman (illustrations)*
This story, told through simple rhymes and appealing watercolor prints, takes us on a lunchtime trek across nine states, two Canadian Provinces and 11 countries. Children from around the world are shown eating food that ranges from curry to tempura to fruit salad. It's a great introduction to a variety of cultures.

To Market, to Market *By Anne Miranda and Janet Stevens (illustrations)*
This is a take-off on a classic Mother Goose fairy tale. Instead of a traditional market, the woman goes to the grocery store to buy the things she needs for lunch. Just as in the original story, all kinds of unexpected things happen while she shops.

"The greatest revolution in our generation is the discovery that human beings, by changing inner attitudes of their minds, can change the outer aspects of their lives."

WILLIAM JAMES, PSYCHOLOGIST

Ages and
Stages

15 through
17 Months

Ages and Stages

15 through 17 Months

What You'll Discover In This Section . . .

"...when toddlers are immersed in language, they use their language earlier and more efficiently."

KATHY HIRSH-PASEK DEVELOPMENTAL PSYCHOLOGIST

- What's Happening: 15 through 17 Months.
- Activities to Nurture Intellectual Development.
- Activities to Encourage Language Development.
- Activities to Nurture a Love of Music.
- Activities for Psycho-Motor Development.
- Activities for Social-Emotional Development.
- Books to Add to Your Library.

107

"Children have never been very good at listening to their elders, but they have never failed to imitate them."

JAMES BALDWIN, AUTHOR

As your toddler's intellectual capacities continue to develop, she'll continue to spend more and more time simply exploring – perhaps as much as 80 percent of her time – but exploration now takes on a somewhat different flavor. Prior to 15 months, a lot of her exploration was spent on trial-and-error, which gave her an understanding of how certain actions cause certain outcomes. As a result, she is better able to create mental representations of objects and actions and understand the feelings, motivations and intentions of others. What all this means is that she is able to anticipate possible outcomes from her actions. Games in which there are predictable outcomes, therefore, take on a growing importance. She'll love bowling for paper towel rolls or building a house of cards and knocking it down.

During this three-month period, your toddler's language skills will continue to grow. She'll add a few words to her vocabulary each week – usually labels of objects in her of immediate world – and her comprehension will keep growing by leaps and bounds. You'll also hear her play personal language games, imitating the inflection and meter of adult speech in conversations directed to

herself. Feed her interest in words by naming everything around her, and focusing her attention on new things, such as the clouds in the sky or the monkeys at the zoo.

Some of the signs of negativism that began in the previous three months begin to become part of your toddler's daily routine as she understands – and then questions – social conventions. She may not want to get dressed, for example, or may refuse to get into her car seat. Remember that toddlers are not being purposefully difficult; they are simply showing an increased understanding of the rules we live by, and coming to grips with how their ability to do things sometimes fits in, and sometimes doesn't.

Remember that with increased independence comes increased uncertainty and insecurity. Toddlers at this age often develop fears – some obvious and understandable, such as stranger anxiety, and others not so obvious or understandable, such as fear of going down the bathtub drain. In the face of these fears and conventions, you'll often see toddlers swing rapidly from joy and laughter to tears and anger. Maintain your composure, be consistent in enforcing and explaining social conventions and be a good role model; she's still looking to you for cues on how to respond emotionally. One good trick for handling negativism is to give your toddler choices: "Would you like to wear the red shirt or the blue shirt?" "Do you want to climb into your car seat or should I lift you in?" Choices let her feel like she's in control.

Along with her burgeoning sense of self, your toddler is beginning to understand concepts of ownership. You'll find her being highly possessive of things she believes belong to her – which can range from a particular cup to a particular seat on the couch. Ownership is a new and important concept, and this behavior should not been seen as selfish. The ability to understand the notion of sharing is still about a year away.

Your toddler is now walking with much more confidence. Although she is most likely still walking with her feet spread wide and continues to fall on occasion, you can see improvements in her posture, balance and movements. Keep in mind, however, that she is not yet able to completely master these skills, and many of the things we take for granted, such as holding a cup while walking, are still out of her reach. Toddlers of this age love to climb, but monitor this activity closely; whereas before she might have climbed on the couch or a chair, now she might try to climb on a table, counter or to some other dangerous spot. Take her to the park, stand nearby and let her climb the ladder to the big slide.

In addition to large motor skills, fine motor skills increase at this point, as well. Let her practice these skills with toys such as puzzles (with large handles to grasp) and foods such as peas and Cheerios.

WHAT'S HAPPENING: 15 THROUGH 17 MONTHS

Perception & Cognition	Vocalizations & Language	Social-Emotional	Motor
• Begins to engage in spontaneous functional play, *e.g.*, she'll pretend to have a conversation while talking on a toy phone. • Loves to test cause-and-effect relationships, *e.g.*, flushing toilets or closing doors. • Loves to play with spatial relationships, *e.g.*, pouring water from one container into another. • Problem-solving skills are exercised constantly, as she figures out how to open drawers or zip up jackets. • Places objects in containers and then removes them. • Begins to anticipate events, such as the tickle at the end of "This Little Piggy."	• Begins to echo the words of others. • Begins to label familiar objects and people, but continues to over-generalize labels for categories of objects. • Imitates common animal sounds. • Manipulates her voice so that sounds mirror adult conversations. • Comprehension of words continues to far outpace production.	• Is able to recognize herself in a mirror. • Displays a wide range of emotional states in a very short period of time, *e.g.*, elation, anger, sadness. • Begins to respond differently to different caretakers, often demonstrating more *negativism* to caregivers to whom she is closest. • Begins to understand and be able to comply with adult rules and conventions. • Feels empathy for others, and will often offer some type of assistance to others in need.	• Is able to stack two blocks. • Is able to grasp a crayon and scribble. • Walks everywhere; would rather push a stroller or shopping cart than ride in one. • Begins to be able to manipulate puzzle pieces that have large handles.

ACTIVITIES FOR BABIES FROM 15 THROUGH 17 MONTHS
ACTIVITIES TO NURTURE INTELLECTUAL DEVELOPMENT

Activity	Description of the Activity	Benefit
Fall Foliage	If you are fortunate to live where the seasons change, find a tree near your home and snap a picture of it during each season. Take a summer picture out to the tree in winter, or a fall picture out in summer so you can see how the tree has changed.	A ritual that teaches cause-and-effect relationships and strengthens memory skills.
Frozen Bubbles	If you live in a cold climate, try blowing bubbles outside on a very cold day. The bubbles will freeze. Pop them, look at them, talk about the rainbows you see in them and discuss how frozen bubbles are different from non-frozen bubbles. If you don't have bubbles, create a mist by blowing your warm breath into the cold air.	A perfect lesson in cause-and-effect relationships that also teaches size and shape concepts.
Lazy Susan	Place a variety of unbreakable objects on a "Lazy Susan." Show your toddler how to spin it, and watch what happens. Try spinning the turntable fast, then try slow. Try placing the objects near the middle, or near the outer edge.	Develops understanding of cause-and-effect relationships and exercises fine motor skills.
Match That Tiger	Tape pictures of wild animals on the wall. Now take all of her stuffed animals, and place them under the pictures they match — the teddy bears beneath the grizzly bear, the elephants beneath the elephants and so on. Which picture ended up having the most stuffed animals?	Reinforces sorting, counting and categorization skills.
Matisse in the Making	Give your toddler a smock, a safe area in which to paint, lots of paper, washable paints and a set of paintbrushes she can easily hold. Display her masterpieces throughout the house.	Builds pre-writing and self-confidence skills.
Mountains of Paper	Add non-toxic food coloring to water in a spray bottle. Add a good measure of the mixture to some old newspaper and soak to the point where the paper becomes moldable dough. Use it to create mountainscapes, or even moonscapes. Help her spray even more of the water on the paper to color it.	A great lesson in cause-and-effect relationships that also inspires imaginative play.
One Step, Two	Count the steps to the second floor as you go up and down the stairs; make a game of this, building the excitement as you near the top, or even counting down to the end. Monitor closely for safety.	Teaches number concepts and develops gross motor skills.

Activity	Description of the Activity	Benefit
Page by Page	In a three-ring binder, create a book of things by gluing pictures on each page. Ask your toddler what should go on the first page, maybe suggesting something like horses. Then sit down and go through magazines and cut out pictures of horses. The next day do something else, like clouds, mountains, or bicycles. The result will be a special book you can enjoy for months to come.	Develops categorization, vocabulary and pre-literacy skills, and inspires imaginative play.
Sock Balls	As you prepare to do your laundry, roll pairs of socks into a ball. Let her toss them into the laundry basket. Count each one as it goes in the basket.	A ritual that teaches number concepts and develops both fine and gross motor skills.
Simon Says, in the Mirror	Stand in front of a full-length mirror, with your toddler in front of you. Play a game of Simon Says, demonstrating each movement for her. Be sure to touch your nose, eyes, ears and so on, but add silly gestures, too — such as arm-waving and goofy sounds.	Exercises both fine and gross motor skills and develops self-awareness.
Sorting Baskets	Take three small laundry baskets and tape pictures of your toddler's favorite toys to the inside bottoms. For example, in one basket there could be a picture of stuffed animals, in another a picture of blocks, and so on. At clean-up time, have your toddler help you by sorting her toys into the appropriate baskets.	A ritual that builds pre-literacy and categorization skills, and encourages social skills.
Squeak and Find	Play hide-and-seek with one of your toddler's favorite squeaky toys. Start by showing her two toys — the squeaky one and another toy of a similar size. Place them both under a blanket, and ask your toddler to find the squeaky toy. Give her a clue (if she needs it) by squeaking the toy under the blanket.	Reinforces concept of object permanence, and strengthens memory and counting skills.
What Should I Wear Today?	As you get your toddler dressed, talk about the color of everything you are putting on her. Describe how you are going to choose red socks to go with her red shirt, and how a blue sweater would look good over her blue dress.	Fosters language learning, teaches color concepts and provides practice in sequencing.

Activity	Description of the Activity	Benefit
Do You See What I See?	Play the classic game of "Do you see what I see?" (where one person says "I see something that's big and red" and the other people guess — fire truck, ball, etc.). Let your toddler be the one to pick out something. Exaggerate the game by naming a long list of incorrect objects before you give the right answer.	Reinforces language development, builds vocabulary and provides practice in problem-solving.
Hold Your Tongue	When your child is excited about telling you something and gets stuck as she tries to get the words out, hold your tongue. Let her struggle to find the words. Once she's finished, repeat what she's said and elaborate on it.	Encourages language skills, builds confidence, encourages social skills and lets her know you are listening.
Fast & Slow	Start with a rhyme — ones that focus on repeated alliteration, such as Peter Piper, are especially good. Repeat it slowly, then say it as fast as you can. Do this several times, mixing up the speed.	Reinforces language development and inspires imitative play.
Full or Empty?	Place two empty laundry baskets on the floor. Add some toys to one of the baskets and describe for her the difference between empty and full. Now, transfer the toys from the one basket to the other, until all the toys are in the second basket and the first basket is empty.	Teaches counting skills and introduces concepts of empty and full.
My Own Recipes	Keep a "recipe book" with your toddler's cooking toys. Put a "carpentry book" with the hammering toys. Add a "script" to the dress up box. Teach her that almost every game you play can be made even more fun with a book. Use catalog pictures to create her special workbooks.	Builds pre-literacy skills, inspires imitative play and provides practice with symbols.
Near or Far?	Sit next to each other on the floor, with your backs to the wall. Roll a ball out from between your legs and help your toddler do the same. Ask her which one is near and which one is far.	Develops fine and gross motor skills and introduces the concepts of near and far.

Activity	Description of the Activity	Benefit
My Own Art Gallery	Create a space in your toddler's room for an art gallery. A small bulletin board works very well. Hang a series of pictures, and every day go over to name the object in each picture — tree, mommy, dog, and so on. Change the pictures frequently.	A useful ritual for introducing new concepts and words that also provides practice with symbols and strengthens memory skills.
Rainbow Book	Make a rainbow book by placing colored construction paper in a three-ring binder, in the order of the colors of a rainbow (red, orange, yellow, green, blue and violet). Write the names of each color on each page. On the final page of the book, draw a complete rainbow.	Builds pre-literacy skills, develops fine motor skills and introduces color concepts.
Squash	Find a comfortable place on the floor. Lay down and have your toddler sit on the floor between your legs. Relax, and begin naming different vegetables: tomato, potato, carrot. Then, in an animated voice, say "Squash!" while you bring your legs together and gently squash her.	Builds vocabulary and develops gross motor skills.
Why This Shirt?	Create a ritual around dressing time by explaining your choice of clothes. "We'll wear this sweater today because it is going to be COLD." "We are going to wear the fancy shirt today because we are going to a FORMAL party."	Builds vocabulary and demonstrates cause-and-effect relationships (by linking the weather to what clothes to wear).
Tortoise and the Hare	Take a walk in the garden until you come upon a snail. Watch her for a little while. Next, look up in the sky and find a flying bird. Talk about which one of the two creatures is moving faster and which is moving slower.	Fosters language learning and introduces concepts of fast and slow.
Yum, That's Good!	While having lunch, talk about the bananas, peas and apples. Describe the taste and texture, (e.g., sweet or sour, crunchy or soft). This is an especially good time to compare and contrast.	Introduces new words and concepts.

Activity	Description of the Activity	Benefit
Cinderella	Stand next to the stairs with your toddler and recite the following rhyme. As you recite the line about going upstairs, holding your toddler's hand, take a big step up to the first stair. On the next line, take that step back down: *Cinderella, dressed in yellow* *Went to find her bow* *She went upstairs to curl her hair* *Then came back down below*	Reinforces language development and exercises gross motor skills.
Put Your Little Foot	Standing in the kitchen — or wherever you would like — recite the following verse. Follow the lead of the words: *Put your little foot, Put your little foot* *Put your little foot right here* *Put your little foot, Put your little foot* *Put your little foot right here* *Turn around and around,* *Clap you hands, make a sound* *Turn around and around* *Show the spot you have found*	Reinforces language development, musical awareness and gross motor skills.
Skip to My Lou	As you sing "Skip to my Lou," skip with your toddler. When you get to "dar-ling," stop and give her a huge hug and kiss: *Skip, skip, skip to my Lou* *Skip, skip, skip to my Lou* *Skip, skip, skip to my Lou* *Skip to my Lou, my dar-ling*	Reinforces language development, musical awareness and gross motor skills.

Activity	Description of the Activity	Benefit
Slowly, Slowly	Sit in a chair with your toddler on your lap facing away from you. Make long slow circles on the top of her head as you recite this rhyme. On the last line, move your hands down her arms, and end in a big hug: *Slowly, slowly, very slowly* *Creeps the garden snail* *Slowly, slowly, very slowly* *Up the wooden rail*	Reinforces language development and musical awareness while providing a sense of comfort.
The Mouse	Sit on the floor and recite the following rhyme, as quickly as you can. Scratch the floor to make the scurrying sounds of the mouse: *There* *I saw a mouse run ... and ... and there .... there* *He ran down the clock and into a hole* *That was under a crack in the stair*	Reinforces language development, musical awareness and fine motor skills.
The Snail	Recite the following rhyme, as slowly as you can. Stretch out the word "stretch " as long as you can: *I saw a snail* *He sure moved slow* *He'd scrunch together* *And stretch way out* *Yep! That's the way he'd go.*	Reinforces language development, musical awareness and fine motor skills.

Activity	Description of the Activity	Benefit
To Market	Try reciting this rhyme as you're getting ready to go to the market, or if you are reading a book with pictures of food: *To market, to market* *To buy some good fruit* *Home again, home again* *Rooty, toot, toot!* You can expand the main chorus of the rhyme with something such as: *To market, to market* *To buy some good spinach* *Home again, home again* *Now we are finished.*	Reinforces language development and musical awareness and builds pre-literacy skills.

ACTIVITIES FOR PSYCHO-MOTOR DEVELOPMENT

Activity	Description of the Activity	Benefit
Eat Your Peas	Although you may be trying to get her to use a spoon at mealtimes, give her some peas or corn as a snack and encourage her to eat with her fingers. Show her how to pick up the food between her thumb and forefinger.	Strengthens grasping skills and encourages social skills.
Let's Go Bowling III	Line up three empty paper towel rolls. From just a few inches away, let your toddler roll a beach ball into the rolls, knocking them down. As she masters the skill, move slightly farther from the rolls and add a few more.	Builds fine and gross motor skills and strengthens self-confidence.
My Hat is Off to You	Sit on the floor with your toddler facing you. Place a baseball hat on your head. Give her one, and show her how to wear it. Now, try turning the bill so that it's facing to the right, to the left and finally to the back.	Develops spatial skills, encourages social skills and inspires imitative play.

Activity	Description of the Activity	Benefit
Piggy Bank	Get a fun piggy bank, and help her put quarters into the slot. As she masters the quarters, move on to nickels, pennies and finally dimes.	Develops fine motor and counting skills, and teaches concepts of size and shape.
Rice Balls	Wash your hands, cook some sticky rice, and show her how to roll her own rice balls. Serve them for dinner.	Builds fine motor and social skills, and inspires imitative play.
Teddy Train	Tie three small boxes together using a short piece of string. Tie one long piece of string to the first box. Place one stuffed animal in each box. Now, pull! Monitor closely, and properly dispose of the string when you are finished.	Strengthens gross motor and counting skills, and sparks the imagination.
The Magic Carpet	Have your toddler sit on a towel or her blanket. Show how to her hold onto the sides, and pull her around the house as if she's on a magic carpet ride.	Demonstrates cause-and-effect relationships and develops fine and gross motor skills.
The Shrinking Ball	Sit on the floor with your legs spread and your toddler directly across from you. Roll a small beach ball back and forth. As she masters this skill, move to a slightly smaller ball, and work your way progressively smaller to a ball the size of a golf ball.	Develops fine motor skills and introduces concepts of larger and smaller.
The Sponge Squeeze	Place three sponges in a pail of water (either outside or on the kitchen floor). Show her how the sponges soak up the water when you place them in the pail. Show her how to squeeze them out and start all over again.	A lesson in cause-and-effect relationships that exercises hand and arm muscles.
Toe the Line	Draw a straight line approximately five feet long with some chalk on the sidewalk. Show her how to walk along it, then let her try. As she masters this, make the line a little longer and try it again. As she gets even better, let her draw the line.	Exercises strength and balance and develops fine motor skills.

Activity	Description of the Activity	Benefit
Eye Level Art at Floor Level	As your toddler becomes an artist, be sure to display her work, especially at a level where she can admire it. Lower drawers in the kitchen are a great place to do this, because she can see the work, you are in and out of that room all day long and the art can often be easily removed from these cabinets.	Develops fine motor skills and gives you a perfect way to encourage and reward artistic endeavors.
Food Art	Make your toddler a sandwich in the shape of a teddy bear by using a cookie cutter to cut the bread. Add nuts or raisins to make eyes and a nose.	Makes lunchtime a fun time and inspires imaginative play.
Hugs and Kisses	When your toddler's on your lap, give her a huge hug and say the word "hug." Give her a big kiss and say "kiss." Try a "peck on the cheek," a "fishy kiss" or a "bear hug."	Reinforces language development and pro-social skills.
Meet Me at My Place	Even toddlers like to have their own safe place. Create a special place in the house with pillows and some favorite toys and books, and make it her place. Encourage her to go there for special moments or quiet time.	Provides her with a sense of security and self-assurance and encourages emotional regulation.
The Growing Mirror	Tape pictures of your toddler at different ages on a full-length mirror on the back of a door. Periodically stop by the mirror and have your toddler compare the way she looked at birth, three months, six months, etc., to how she looks now.	Fosters self-awareness and strengthens memory.
Where Does That Eye Go?	Have your toddler lay down on a long piece of drawing paper. Draw the outline of her body, then let her fill in the different parts of her body, including hair, eyes, nose, etc.	Fosters self-awareness and teaches size and shape concepts
Where's My Baby?	Pretend you can't see your toddler for a moment. Say, "Where's Emily?" and look around the room and right past her. She'll happily protest — "Here I am!" After a short moment, go over to her, hug her and say, "There you are!"	Fosters self-awareness and strengthens memory.

Books to Add to Your 15- through 17-Month-Old's Library

1-2 Peek-a-Boo! *By Sonja Lamut*
We can't recommend this type book, or this book in particular, strongly enough for toddlers. A short book that will hold your baby's attention, it introduces an important concept (numbers) and it motivates toddlers to finish the thought by having them complete the number sequence.

A is for Africa *By Ifeoma Onyefulu*
Onyefulu, a native of Nigeria, provides a unique and beautiful introduction to the alphabet by taking us on a photographic sojourn of life in her homeland. The photographs are beautiful and provide even the youngest children a different set of associations for the letters of the alphabet.

All the Colors of the Earth *By Sheila Hamanaka*
This is a book dedicated to the diversity of the world and the people in it. The artwork is striking, and the portrayal of children from around the world is a very nice way to introduce your toddler to the wonders of the entire world.

Alphabite! A Funny Feast from A to Z *By Charles Reasoner and Vicky Hardt (illustration)*
Who's been taking bites out of all of the vegetables? You have to get through the entire ABCs – bitten, nibbled and gobbled though they are – to solve the mystery.

The Big Book of Beautiful Babies *By David Ellwand*
This wonderful book is filled with black and white pictures of babies experiencing every emotional state – from glee to despair. For toddlers who are just beginning to understand the mental states of others, this is a book to cherish.

Big Dog ... Little Dog *By Philip Eastman*
We think this book is one of the best for teaching opposites. The two dogs, illustrated in bright and bold drawings, are opposite in just about every way you can imagine, and they let you know it. Even so, the dogs turn out to be the best of friends.

Blue, Blue, and Yellow Too *By Biruta Akerbergs-Hansen*
Color, language, fine motor coordination and animals are all featured in this book from the National Geographic Society. Learn about green chameleons and brown bats through catchy rhymes and fun pop-up tabs.

Blue Hat, Green Hat *By Sandra Boynton*
This cute little board book teaches all the colors in a simple story about the social conventions of getting dressed. The turkey, who we love, and who never seems to get anything quite right, punctuates the point on every page.

Brian Wildsmith's ABC *By Brian Wildsmith*
This book was originally introduced over 30 years ago, and has remained a favorite because of its ability to introduce the alphabet to a new generation of readers and celebrate the artistic spirit all at the same time. The images are sure to grab your toddler's attention while she learns all about letters.

Down in the Garden Alphabet Book *By Anne Geddes*
This beautiful book is the sister companion for Anne Gedde's "Down in the Garden Counting Book." Together, the two make for a great early introduction to numbers and letters.

Giving Thanks: A Native American Good Morning Message *By Chief Jake Swamp and Erwin Printup, Jr. (illustration)*
This book is based upon a traditional Mohawk message of thanks to Mother Earth for all of the gifts she has provided us. The text of this tale is brief, and the color spreads do justice to the gratitude that is being offered. These important themes make this book a welcome addition to any toddler's library.

Guess How Much I Love You *By Sam McBratney and Anita Jeram (illustration)*
One of our favorites for fathers and sons. This great bedtime game has Big Nutbrown Hare besting each of Little Nutbrown Hare's statements of love. The interactions are wonderful, and a sweet way to get your toddler to bed.

Hanukkah Lights, Hanukkah Nights *By Leslie Kimmelman and John Himmelman (illustration)*
This is a very good introduction to the holiday of Hanukkah. It's a book that you can move through quickly, starting with the lighting of the shammash and moving through each of the eight nights of Hanukkah.

If You Were My Bunny *By David McPhail and Kate McMullan (illustration)*
What do a bunny, a cub, a kitten, a puppy and a baby all have in common? Mothers who love them very much. The message is clear in this lovely story: babies of all species are cherished by their own kind.

Lots of Moms *By Shelley Rotner and Sheilla Kelly (illustration)*
Moms come in all shapes, sizes and colors, and this book proves it in a surprisingly realistic look at the many roles that mothers play and the many ways that mothers love. This is a lovely cross-cultural look at motherhood.

Mouse Count *By Ellen Walsh*
This is one of the better counting books we've ever come across. The text is simple and the graphics are engaging. In this story, some very sly mice get the better of a hungry snake. Toddlers are given a lesson in counting to 10 as the snake places the mice in a jar, and then they are given a lesson in counting backward from 10 as the clever mice all escape.

Mr. Putter and Tabby Pick the Pears *By Cynthia Rylant and Arthur Howard (illustration)*
One in the terrific series of Mr. Putter books, and one of the most hilarious. Mr. Putter is a little old man who wants a little bit of pear jelly, but he can't manage to pick the pears the way he used to. With help from his fine cat, Tabby, he comes up with an innovative approach toddlers will love.

My Little ABC Book *By Bob Staake*
The first alphabet book for the computer generation, this is a stylish interpretation of a classic alphabet primer. Staake's images are an exciting way to introduce the fun of learning the alphabet.

One Yellow Lion: Fold-Out Fun with Numbers, Colors and Animals *By Matthew Van Fleet*
This is a very clever book that covers a wide variety of concepts, including numbers, shapes, colors and animals. It's a very interactive read, since each page has a hidden object and toddlers are invited to guess what is hidden behind the fold-out pages.

The Rooster's Gift *By Pam Conrad and Erric Beddows (illustration)*
Oh what joy to be able to make the sun rise just by speaking a powerful Cot Cot Cot. That is just the power that one young rooster believes he has, and it is only a slight miscalculation that makes him realize it isn't quite so. His spirits are lifted, however, when his little sister – the little hen – lets him know that doing something well is a gift unto itself.

Sleep Tight, Mrs. Ming *By Sharon Jennings and Levert Mireille (illustration)*
It's bedtime, and in the third Mrs. Ming book, Jeremiah and his old friend, Mrs. Ming, are having a hard time falling asleep. Together, they come up with an amusing solution to their problem, and they eventually get to sleep. A perfect book to use as a bedtime ritual.

The Squiggle *By Carole Schaefer and Pierr Morgan (illustration)*
It's only a piece of string on the sidewalk, but in the hands of a little girl with a vivid imagination, it's so much more – it's the moon, it's a dragon, it's fireworks. This simple book is a great celebration of the imagination.

Ten Flashing Fireflies *By Phileomon Sturges and Anna Vojtech (illustration)*
The night is dark, and the sky echoes past summers. The fireflies circle, but they seem to slowly, and strangely, disappear. Suddenly, they begin to reappear in a jar, as a boy and girl capture them. As the 10 fireflies disappear from the sky and make their appearance in the jar, you can count up to 10, and back down again.

Time for Bed *By Mem Fox and Jane Dyer (illustration)*
Babies of all different kinds adorn these pages. It's bedtime, and not all of them want to go to bed. But mom is there, cuddling each of them, rocking them in her arms until finally, at last, each and every one dozes off. It can help make a toddler who's not quite ready to go to sleep do just that.

When You Were a Baby *By Ann Jonas*
A great story that reminds your four-year-old how much he's learned and how much he can do. Your child will come away feeling just like a big kid should feel: on top of the world!

Where Are You Going Manyoni? *By Catherine Stock*
Each morning, at the crack of dawn, Manyoni walks along the Limpopo river, two hours in all, to get to school. Along the way, she passes the stunning scenery – the wildlife of Zimbabwe. The story is simple, and young children will love the animals and the beautiful water colors.

White Rabbit's Color Book *By Alan Baker*
There are many books that teach your toddler about colors, but not a whole lot that teach about how colors can mix together to produce some fun results. This books teaches the concept quite nicely, as white rabbit jumps from bucket to bucket, mixing paints into some pretty interesting combinations.

The Z was Zapped *By Chris Van Allsburg*
Van Allsburg is a two-time Caldecott medal winner, and it shows on every page of this wonderful alphabet book. In this version, whole adventures happen to the letters. The "A" is in an avalanche and the "Z" get zapped.

Ages and
Stages

18 through
20 Months

Ages and Stages

18 through 20 Months

"Sow a thought, and you reap an act;

Sow an act, and you reap a habit;

Sow a habit, and you reap a character;

Sow a character, and you reap a destiny."

CHARLES READE, JOURNALIST

What You'll Discover In This Section

- What's Happening: 18 through 20 Months.

- Activities to Nurture Intellectual Development.

- Activities to Encourage Language Development.

- Activities to Nurture a Love of Music.

- Activities for Psycho-Motor Development.

- Activities for Social-Emotional Development.

- Books to Add to Your Library.

121

"Children need a flood of information, a banquet, a feast."
MARTHA PIERSON, NEUROBIOLOGIST

For many families, the time starting around 18 months marks the beginning of some of the most extraordinary and wonderful developments of childhood. One of these developments comes through loud and clear: a major jump in your toddler's ability to speak and understand words (see **Language** section, page 35, for details). Although the number of words your toddler has been producing has probably been growing steadily, there is a noticeable increase in how much and how often he is now speaking to you. He easily names lots of objects and begins to add verbs and adjectives to his sentences. You may hear a noun and a verb being linked together during this period, such as "Go park," or "Want juice," and will sometimes hear the same word linked with everything – "big dog," "big chair," "big elephant." Keep reading to him, and don't be afraid to read books that might seem to be a little too old for him. He'll take what he can now, and will quickly grow into the vocabulary and complexity.

One seemingly paradoxical development that comes with the leap in vocabulary is a struggle to produce words; some toddlers might almost appear to be stuttering. As toddlers learn more words and have a wider choice of options from which to choose, they sometimes have a hard time finding just the right word.

Sometimes you might hear him try a number of words, then finally settle on one he likes. Be supportive by giving him some time to find the right word on his own, and stepping in only after you think frustration might be nearing.

The intellectual developments of the 15- through 17-month range become stronger and stronger after 18 months. His understanding of cause-and-effect relationships, for example, and the ability to predict outcomes, gets even more reliable. As a result, you'll often see him stopping and pondering what to do next rather than having the immediate and spontaneous reaction you might have seen earlier. Continue to give him toys and activities that center on one event causing another, and as you go through your daily routine, highlight the order of what will happen. As you get dressed in the morning, for example, talk about how first you're going to get dressed, then have breakfast, then get in the car to go to the park. Also, give him short requests that involve two or three steps, *e.g.*, "Can you please bring me a piece of paper, and then get your crayons. We can draw a picture."

His ability to create mental representations of objects and events has been growing constantly, and at this age, you get a wonderful result – the beginnings of imaginative play. Up to this point, play is still not quite imaginative – he may be using objects in a functional way (*e.g.*, talking on a toy telephone) but he's just now beginning to create play worlds in which he can incorporate those functional objects in imaginative ways. This is the perfect moment to introduce dress-up clothes, play food and doll houses, and watch as he becomes a prince, a baker or the father of the make-believe family. He'll also continue to enjoy imitating the functional things adults do all day, such as cook, drive, talk on the phone, fix the toaster, open the mail, etc.

Negativism continues to hang around. He is now strongly aware that he is a capable and independent person who wants to make choices, do things on his own and do it his own way. He understands many social conventions and understands that he can question them. Again, this is a good thing; within this understanding, he will mature into a loving, self-confident and capable person. During this phase, he will look to you for comforting, perhaps gesturing that he wants to be picked up, only to have him immediately squiggle in an effort to be placed back on the ground. Be patient as he pushes and pulls, and help him understand which behaviors he is capable of and which behaviors are unacceptable.

Up until 18 months, toddlers play with each other in a way that scientists call parallel: they play in the same physical proximity to each other, but have no real interaction. You'll often see two 12-month-olds sitting back to back, happily playing and totally ignoring each other. At around 18 months, however, you can see your toddler and another child begin to subtly interact with each other as they play. If you observe closely, you can make out a type of silent dance between the two, as they begin adding suggestions for what their friends should do, or injecting some elements of their own play into their playmate's games. This type of interaction marks a significant precursor to the full-fledged shared play that will emerge after the second year.

With increased strength and balance in walking, dancing becomes a favorite activity. Your toddler will love to practice twirls, pirouettes and stomping. Put on some music and let him go! Add some instruments or scarves to twirl, and his play gets even more fun. Fine motor skills are also improving dramatically, and he is able to hold kitchen utensils to the point where he can now feed himself. Bear with the mess, and encourage his autonomy.

Parents tell it like it is:

"Kira loves to sit in the car seat and keep a running dialogue for us. Sometimes her choice of words just makes us laugh. Last week she said, "Mom I'm not 'comforter' in this seat."
MAUREEN HOUSMAN, MOTHER OF KIRA AND LEAH

What's Happening: 18 through 20 Months

Perception & Cognition	Vocalizations & Language	Social-Emotional	Motor
• Is able to point to his ears, eyes and nose when asked.	• Continues to label as many things in his environment as he can.	• Often becomes upset when a parent or caregiver leaves the room.	• Able to feed himself using a spoon.
• Begins to refer to himself by name.	• Begins to add suffixes to words to make plurals and to create past tense forms, such as "cars" and "goed."	• Becomes much more sensitive, and feelings are often very easily hurt.	• Able to bend over to pick up a toy without falling.
• Imitation of adults becomes a favorite activity.		• Peer communications are mainly visual rather than verbal.	• Able to walk up steps with some assistance.
• Begins to manipulate multiple objects, e.g., if he is holding an object in each hand, and is presented a third, he'll look for a way to hold all three.	• Dramatic increase in the number of words he is producing.	• Takes time to be comfortable in new situations.	• Able to take a few steps backward.
	• Over-generalizes grammatical rules, e.g., saying "thinked" instead of "thought."		• Able to throw a ball overhand.
• Begins to engage in more play that is independent of you and other adults.	• Uses the name of objects to ask for them.		• Able to twist and move to the beat of a song.
• Increasingly likes to test limits.	• Begins to ask what things are called, e.g., asks "whatsat?"		

"Experience is never limited, and it is never complete."

HENRY JAMES, AUTHOR

ACTIVITIES FOR BABIES FROM 18 THROUGH 20 MONTHS
ACTIVITIES TO NURTURE INTELLECTUAL DEVELOPMENT

Activity	Description of the Activity	Benefit
Alphabet Soup Art	Dip alphabet blocks with raised letters in water-based paint. Let your toddler press the blocks onto construction paper to make an alphabet soup design. Name each of the letters.	Introduces letter concepts, and develops fine motor and counting skills.
Animal Crackers	Place a handful of animal crackers on a plate, and help your toddler move them into piles of lions, tigers, bears and so on. When you're finished, count each pile to see which animal wins.	Builds categorization and counting skills and inspires imaginative play.
Backpack Safari	Go on an imaginary safari, letting your toddler pack everything you need into a backpack. After you're packed, pretend to march off to your destination. Once you've marched around the room and "arrived," ask your toddler if he remembered to pack items that are in his backpack, and encourage him to pull them out.	Develops memory capacities and inspires imaginative play.
The Dinner Party	Help your daughter throw a dinner party for some of her favorite stuffed toys. Pick a group of toys that are all the same (*e.g.*, all teddy bears), and pick one exception. Ask her which party guest is different from all the others.	Strengthens categorization and social skills.
Freeform Pancakes	Make a freeform pancake for breakfast. Ask your toddler what he thinks it looks like.	Teaches size and shape concepts and inspires imaginative play.
Growing Sponges	Let a few sponges dry out over night; white sponges work best. Fill three small bowls with non-toxic food coloring, then place each of the dried sponges in the bowl.	A real-world bit of magic that demonstrates cause-and-effect relationships and teaches color concepts and counting skills.
Hoagies	Using some brown construction paper, cut 6" by 6" squares. Do the same with tan, orange and white paper. Now make a sandwich, with the brown paper as the bread, the orange and white as the cheese, the tan as the turkey, and so on. Dig in!	Sparks imaginative play and builds an understanding of sequential relationships.

Activity	Description of the Activity	Benefit
Making Menus	Create a menu for breakfast, lunch and even dinner, by taping pictures of some of your toddler's favorite foods onto a piece of paper. At mealtime, let him make his dining selection by pointing to the food he wants.	A comforting social ritual that reinforces the link between objects and symbols and teaches decision-making skills.
One Nose, Two Ears	Stand behind your toddler in front of a full-length mirror. Point to his nose, and say, "One nose." Point to your nose and say, "One nose." Move on to ears, eyes, etc., counting the proper number as you go.	Develops counting skills while reinforcing self-awareness.
Oobleck	Have your toddler help you mix a batch of cornstarch and water. Add food coloring, if you like. This concoction — better known as Oobleck — makes a solid when rolled, and turns to liquid when you let it sit. It also makes a great sound if you slap it.	A great lesson in cause-and-effect relationships and a unique tactile experience.
Out They Go	Use a large cardboard tube from a roll of gift-wrap. Show your toddler how to drop small toys through the hole and watch them come out the other end. Tip the tube at different angles to show how this changes the way the toys move.	A great lesson in object permanence and cause-and-effect relationships that also develops fine motor skills.
Mixing Paint	Use one of your toddler's most colorful toys as a model. Choose one of the colors, and mix water-based paints until you match the color on the toy. Draw a sketch of the toy on a piece of paper and fill it in with the proper color.	A lesson in color perception and cause-and-effect relationships that also develops fine motor skills.
Rabbit in the Hat	Place three of your toddler's favorite toys in a hat. Quietly remove one of the toys, then let him search through the hat, and ask him which of the toys is missing.	Strengthens memory and object permanence skills.
Race Cars	Place a large piece of cardboard at an angle and show your toddler how to roll small toy cars down the ramp. Once he gets into it, change the angle of the ramp, and talk about how the car goes faster or slower.	Demonstrates cause-and-effect relationships and the power of gravitational forces.

Activity	Description of the Activity	Benefit
Spritzing	Take your toddler out with you when it's time to water the yard. Show him how you can make the water dance. Show him how you can make it sprinkle. Show him how, if you do it just right, you can make a rainbow.	Demonstrates cause-and-effect relationships, develops fine motor skills and teaches size and shape concepts.
She Saw a Seashell	If you live near a beach, go on a seashell hunt. Once you've had a chance to clean the shells, start sorting them. Try sorting by size, color and texture.	Builds categorization and fine motor skills.
Sink or Float	Put a metal spoon in a large plastic bowl filled with water. Next try a piece of aluminum foil, and a piece of wood. Talk about what floats and what sinks.	Demonstrates cause-and-effect relationships, fosters language learning and teaches concept of buoyancy.
Stringing Beads	Place some large — large enough not to pose a choking hazard — colored beads into containers. Start by stringing a very simple pattern, *e.g.*, large round blue beads first, square red ones next. Continue the pattern a few times, then help your toddler continue it. Eventually, he'll be able to copy patterns on his own, and you can move on to more sophisticated designs.	Teaches color, size and shape concepts and introduces pre-math skills.
Sweet Finger Painting	Add a few drops of food coloring to a few dollops of whipped cream. Let your child paint — and eat — his sweet finger paints.	An edible lesson in colors and shapes that develops fine motor skills.
The Things People Do	Collect magazine pictures of men and women at work. Find farmers, chefs, mothers, etc., and make a book about work. As you read it, describe what the person in the picture is doing, where he does it, and why it's important.	Builds pre-literacy skills, exposes your child to new words and concepts and provides practice with symbols.
This Little Piggy	The "Little Piggy" song is and always has been a great way to make some great personal contact with your toddler. If you count out the piggies as you go, this also becomes a lesson in numbers.	Fosters language learning, develops counting skills and encourages social skills.

ACTIVITIES FOR BABIES FROM 18 THROUGH 20 MONTHS
ACTIVITIES TO NURTURE INTELLECTUAL DEVELOPMENT (CONTINUED)

Activity	Description of the Activity	Benefit
Weighing In	Fill a plastic measuring cup with rice. Let your toddler pick it up to see how heavy it is. Next, fill the measuring cup with cereal, and compare the difference. Try water, flour, noodles, etc.	Demonstrates cause-and-effect relationships and builds pre-math concepts.
What Goes In Here?	Label toy storage places with pictures that match the toys inside. Encourage your toddler to find the toys he wants, and to put his toys away in the correct bins. Clear or opaque storage bins are especially good, because your toddler can see what's inside.	Strengthens memory and social skills and provides practice in linking symbols to objects.
What's on the Calendar?	Have your toddler sit on your lap as you plan out the events of the day on a piece of paper. Let him decide whether you go to the grocery store first, or to the post office.	Strengthens sequencing and memory skills.
Where's the Music Box?	Take your toddler's music box, wind it up, and then hide it somewhere in the room. You may want to start off by letting him see where you hide it, then slowly move to hiding the toy when he isn't watching.	Builds memory and problem-solving skills; provides practice in linking sights and sounds; and develops gross motor skills.

ACTIVITIES TO ENCOURAGE LANGUAGE DEVELOPMENT

Activity	Description of the Activity	Benefit
A Car Says Neigh?	Pretend your car is a horse. As you start driving, say, "Here we go — neigh, neigh." Your toddler will think this is hilarious, and will say, "That's not the sound a car makes!" Express surprise and ask him what sound a car makes.	Fosters language learning, strengthens memory and provides practice in linking sounds to objects.
A Day at the Plant Store	Even if you're not planting, the nursery can be a magical place. Visit the different colored flowers, noticing how they look, how they smell, how tall they are, and even where they like to grow.	Develops vocabulary, color recognition skills and the concepts of big and small.
Blow Me Down	Face each other and practice blowing air from your mouth as if you're trying to blow each other over. Try making funny faces at each other accompanied by funny sounds.	Excellent practice for mouth and facial control (which is necessary to clearly articulate spoken words).

Activity	Description of the Activity	Benefit
Junk Mail	Make a special junk mail box for your toddler. Junk mail offers all kinds of words, pictures and adventures. You can sort the mail, read it and deliver it just like the real post office people.	Develops language and pre-literacy skills and provides practice with symbols.
Sandscript	Smooth out the top of your sandbox, and "write" a story with your toddler. Let him do most of the writing, using his finger or a stick.	Builds awareness that symbols represent letters and words while developing fine motor skills.
One, Two, Three, Tah-Dah	Sit in a relatively dark room with a flashlight in hand. Look around the room and say "One, Two, Three, Tah-Dah." On the final beat, beam the flashlight on an object in the room, and ask your toddler to tell you the name of the object.	Strengthens vocabulary, counting and fine motor skills.
Please Bring Me ...	Name three things in the room, each at a height within your toddler's reach. After you name the objects, ask him to bring you one, then the other, then the last.	Reinforces naming skills and memory capacity.
Row Fast, Row Slow	Start singing "Row, Row, Row Your Boat" at the normal speed. On the second and third verse, pick up the pace. On the fourth, try it slow, then maybe soft.	Fosters language learning and provides practice in manipulating and controlling the voice.
Tiptoe Through the Tulips	Go on a nature walk in a park, on a trail or in the woods. Bring along a field guide (for birds, trees or flowers) and match some of what you see to pictures in the book.	Fosters language learning and communicates the concept that reading is a means of gaining information.
What Did I Forget?	Sing one of your toddler's favorite songs, but leave out a few key words. Let him correct you.	Reinforces vocabulary and memory skills.

Activities for Babies from 18 through 20 Months
Activities to Nurture a Love for Music

Activity	Description of the Activity	Benefit
Clap Your Hands	Stand in an open space and recite the following rhyme. Act out the obvious and make up other movements as you go: *Clap, clap, clap your hands, clap your hands together* *Stamp, stamp, stamp your feet, stamp your feet together* *Clap, clap, clap your hands, clap your hands together* *Stamp, stamp, stamp your feet, stamp your feet together* *Tra la la la*	Reinforces language development, musical awareness and both gross and fine motor skills.
Down With the Lambs	At bedtime, stand with your toddler on the first step of the stairs, and recite the following rhyme. As you say the line about going down, hold your toddler's hand and take a big step down the first step of the stairs. On the next line, take that step back up, and head off to bed for your bedtime ritual: *Down with the lambs* *Up with the lark* *Run to bed children* *Before it gets dark*	Reinforces language development, musical awareness, counting skills and gross motor skills.
I Can Hammer	Sit on the ground with your toddler next to you, feet straight ahead. On the sound of the hammer, tap the ground an appropriate number of times. Increase the number with each new verse: *I can hammer with one hammer* *I can hammer with one hammer* *I can hammer with one hammer* *And hammer all day long*	Reinforces language development, musical awareness, counting concepts and fine motor skills.

ACTIVITIES FOR BABIES FROM 18 THROUGH 20 MONTHS
ACTIVITIES TO NURTURE A LOVE FOR MUSIC (CONTINUED)

Activity	Description of the Activity	Benefit
Jim Along Josie	Hold your toddler's hands and on the command "jump," jump together along with your toddler: *Jump, Jim along, Jim along Josie* *Jump, Jim along, Jim along Joe* *Jump, Jim along, Jim along Josie* *Jump, Jim along, Jim along Joe*	Reinforces language development, musical awareness, gross motor skills and balance.
Soft Drum, Loud Drum	Sit on the floor and gently tap a drum. Now tap harder. Give your toddler a turn, instructing him to hit gently and then hard.	Shows how one object can make two sounds and exercises fine motor skills.
Where is Big Silly John?	Draw faces on your own fingers. Make one look especially silly, and to the melody of "Are You Sleeping?" (also known as "Frere Jacques") sing the rhyme below. Start with your fingers closed, and as each new line is sung, let your toddler lift one of your fingers until he finds the silly face. At the end of the song, tickle him: *Where is big silly John?* *Where is big silly John?* *He's not here!* *He's not here!* *Where can he be hiding?* *Where can he be hiding?* *Here he is!* *Here he is!... And he's going to tickle you!*	Reinforces language development, self-awareness, fine motor skills and emotional identification.

Activities for Babies from 18 through 20 Months
Activities for Psycho-Motor Development

Activity	Description of the Activity	Benefit
Laundry Ball	Turn a rectangular laundry basket on its side. Sit on the floor approximately five feet away from the basket. Find the largest beach ball that will fit into the laundry basket and take turns trying to roll it in. Move farther back as his aim improves.	Strengthens fine motor skills and builds self-confidence.
Basket Animal	Place a laundry basket next to your toddler's crib or bed, and take turns trying to toss in his stuffed animals.	Develops fine motor, counting and memory skills, and builds self-confidence.
Beads on My Shoelaces	Show your toddler how to string large beads on his shoelaces, then lace up his shoes and let him go on a march.	Exercises fine motor skills, teaches color concepts and provides practice in sequencing.
Broad Jump	Place a line of tape on the floor and practice taking a big step over the tape. Once he masters this, have him make a jump over the tape. Next, add a second piece of tape, a few inches apart from the first, and have him broad jump over both of them.	Exercises overall balance and develops the muscles in the legs.
Pasta Necklaces	Make a necklace by stringing large pieces of pasta onto yarn. As his fine motor coordination improves, try doing the same with round cereal. Monitor closely, and properly dispose of string and pasta pieces when you are finished.	Exercises fine motor skills and provides practice in sequencing.
Newspaper Shot Put	Crumple up newspaper into balls and take turns throwing. See who can throw it the farthest, or in a special corner or closest to the wall.	Exercises both fine and gross motor skills and builds confidence.
High Dive	Show your toddler how to jump off a low step. Make sure the ground below is soft, or add a pillow to the spot where he may land.	Helps exercise the muscles in the legs and develops overall balance.
Dance Marathon	Put on some of your favorite dance music and dance the night away! Do the twist, the crawl and the swim, and whatever moves your toddler invents.	A fun exercise that develops muscles and body control.

Activity	Description of the Activity	Benefit
Jumping Beans	If you have a small home trampoline, help your toddler learn to stand and to jump. Hold his hands until he masters the skills, and always monitor closely.	Exercises the legs and develops overall balance while teaching counting, singing, language and number skills.
Ropin' Cowboy	Tie string to a small stuffed animal, and throw it out a few feet. Now reel it back in just like the cowboys do. Monitor closely and properly dispose of string when you are finished.	Demonstrates cause-and-effect relationships, develops both fine and gross motor skills and inspires imaginative play.
Line Up The Blocks	Put a straight line of tape on the floor, about one foot long. Ask your toddler to line up some blocks so that they cover the line. As he gets better at this, try creating a curve in the line.	Exercises fine motor skills, teaches counting skills and provides practice in sequencing.
Paper Strips	Show your toddler how to tear paper strips from construction paper, and let him give it a try. Glue the strips onto a larger piece of paper to make a collage.	Teaches size, shape and color concepts and strengthens fine motor skills.
Red Light, Green Light	Play "Red light, Green light" (the game where your toddler starts and stops according to your command); change the movement to slow walking, spinning or side stepping. Let your toddler have a chance to make you stop and go.	Exercises fine and gross motor skills, and teaches language and social skills.
Roller Pain	Clean out old deodorant rollers and fill with washable paint. It's a clean, fun paint brush alternative.	Exercises fine motor skills and inspires imaginative play.
Sidewinders	Get down on the ground with your toddler and show him how to squirm like a snake. When you get really good, make a pillow obstacle course.	Develops gross motor skills and inspires imaginative play.
Slam Dunk	Place a wastebasket so that the rim of the basket is just beyond your extended arm reach. Have him place a beanbag or favorite stuffed animal in the basket. As he gets good at this, raise the basket slightly so he has to stand on tippy-toes.	Teaches counting skills, exercises fine motor skills and balance and builds confidence.

Activity	Description of the Activity	Benefit
Sticker Shock	Use a pen to divide a piece of construction paper into four sections. Have your toddler practice placing large stickers in each of the four sections. As he gets better, try six sections, and so on.	Exercises fine motor and counting skills.
Strawberry Picking	Visit a strawberry patch and go picking!	Exercises fine and gross motor skills.
Streaming	Cut pieces of streamers (from ribbon, yarn or fabric) approximately two feet in length. Run through the yard, letting the streamers flap behind you. Show your toddler how the streamer follows you as you dance in circles, or creates a flying snake as you wind the streamer in different directions. Monitor closely and properly dispose of string when you are finished.	Demonstrates cause-and-effect relationships and exercises fine and gross motor skills.
Strut Like a Rooster	As you sing "Old MacDonald Had a Farm" walk around like the animals featured in song. Try strutting like a rooster and stamping your foot like a horse.	Develops singing and language development skills, inspires imaginative play and teaches body control.
Big Bubbles	Using a large bubble-maker that can be dipped into a tray of bubbles, show your toddler how to wave the wand through the air to make a big bubble.	Teaches size, shape and color concepts and exercises fine and gross motor skills.
The Flamingo	Hold your toddler's hands and have him balance on one leg. As he grows stronger, provide less and less support until he can finally balance on his own.	Exercises gross motor skills and overall balance.
High Jump	Lay a jump rope on the ground, and have your toddler practice stepping over it. After a few turns, raise the rope approximately two inches off the ground, and let him try it again. Keep going, until he's high jumping.	Exercises gross motor skills and overall balance.
The Watering Pail	Bring a small watering pail out to the garden, and let your toddler fill it up with the garden hose. Tell him the plants are thirsty and encourage him to give them a drink.	Exercises fine motor skills, builds body control and inspires imaginative and imitative play.

Activity	Description of the Activity	Benefit
Touch Your Toes	Show your toddler how to reach down and touch his knees. As his strength increases, move down to the ankles, and eventually, touch those toes. Encourage him to bend from the waist when he can.	Exercises gross motor skills and overall balance and stretches out the muscles.
Toy Muffins: Part 1	Get out a small muffin tin and a pile of small toys. Show your toddler how to place a toy into each cup, then pretend to bake the toys.	Exercises fine motor skills and inspires imaginative play.
Walk in My Footsteps	Start by following your toddler, stepping where he steps, and doing what he does. Switch positions, and, let him walk where you walk. Be sure to take small steps. This game is especially fun at the beach.	Exercises coordination and memory, and inspires imitative play.

ACTIVITIES FOR SOCIAL-EMOTIONAL DEVELOPMENT

Activity	Description of the Activity	Benefit
Happy Face, Sad Face	Draw a sad face on one (old) wooden spoon, and a happy one on another. Play act how each spoon must be feeling, then let him have a turn. Ask him which spoon matches how he's feeling today.	Gives him a way to communicate and understand his feelings.
Family on Tape	Record each member of the family saying a few words. Set out pictures of everyone in the family, then play the words back for your toddler. As you play each voice, ask your toddler to point to the picture of the person who is speaking.	A comforting social ritual that exercises memory skills and provides practice in linking sounds with visual cues.
He Didn't Mean to Do It	The next time your toddler gets a scrape or is the victim of another toddler's actions, explain the difference between an accident and something that happens on purpose. Use the words "accident" and "didn't mean to."	Teaches pro-social skills.
Hokey-Pokey Bath	As you help him step into the bathtub, sing the hokey-pokey song. Put the appropriate limbs in at the appropriate times.	Builds body and musical awareness, and develops fine motor skills.
The Wall of Emotions	Take some pictures of your toddler when he's happy, sad, excited, angry, etc. Tape them to a wall in his room where he can clearly see them. Visit the wall periodically, and ask which one is a happy face, which is a sad face, and so on. You can also use the pictures to help him communicate how he might be feeling.	Teaches recognition of emotions through expressions, develops self-awareness and provides practice with symbols.

Books to Add to Your 18- through 20-Month-Old's Library

All About Where *By Tana Hoban*
A collection of wordless pictures of magical places that will spark endless storytelling by parents and toddlers alike. A perfect way to develop creativity and imagination for years to come.

Alphabatics *By Suse MacDonald*
Have you ever seen a "b" contort itself into the shape of a balloon? How about a "y" become a yak? In this very clever book, toddlers see how letters go with pictures, objects and sounds, and it's done in such a fun way, that learning the alphabet has never been easier.

Alphabet City *By Stephen Johnson*
Is that a "C" in the crack in the sidewalk? A "B" on the side of that building? The letters of the alphabet are found all over a beautiful cityscape in this clever treatment of the alphabet. This book received a 1996 Caldecott Award for its engaging artwork.

And If the Moon Could Talk *By Kate Banks and Georg Hallensleben (illustration)*
A classic bedtime story with a quiet rhyme and a comforting storyline somewhat reminiscent of the classic "Goodnight Moon." A perfect bedtime story.

Color Dance *By Ann Jonas*
Scarves of color flow across the pages, demonstrating for children what happens when you mix red with blue, or yellow with blue. Throw in the effects of white and black for good measure, and the result is a book filled with beautiful images that also happens to teach colors and color combinations.

Colors (Baby Bug Pop-Up Books) *By David Carter*
Bugs of all colors and shapes help toddlers learn about all the colors of the rainbow. The pull tabs are easy for little ones to grasp – both physically and intellectually.

Color Zoo *By Lois Ehlert*
The gloriousness of this little book makes it hard to categorize. It's a book that introduces toddlers to various colors, but it's also an animal book and an imagination book. It can be read on so many levels that it will hold your child's interest for years.

Dumpling Soup *By Jama Rattigan and Lillian Hsu-Flanders (illustration)*
Marisa lives with her family in Hawaii, and it's time to prepare for the New Year's celebration. This is a special year, because it is the first year that Marisa is old enough to help make "mandoo," the traditional dumplings. Relatives descend upon the house, bringing cultural backgrounds from such diverse countries as Japan, Korea and England.

The Gifts of Kwanzaa *By Synthia Saint James and Abby Levine (illustration)*
Saint James walks through the traditions of the Kwanzaa celebration, moving day by day through each night of the holiday. A well-written introduction to Kwanzaa with clean, strong images toddlers will love.

Good Night, Sleep Tight *By Penelope Lively and Adriano Gon (illustration)*
Sometimes when you lie down in bed, no matter how hard you try, your stuffed animal friends are just not ready to go to sleep. On those occasions, there is not much else to do but to go on adventures with them. That is exactly what happens as a little girl goes hopping off with her friends the frog, lion and cat. In the end, sleep overtakes them all. The clean drawings and bright colors will certainly capture your toddler's attention, and the wind down to bedtime will help you create a nice ritual.

How Many, How Many, How Many *By Rick Walton and Cynthia Halperin (illustration)*
This is one of our favorite books about number concepts. It seamlessly moves from classic nursery rhymes to names of seasons to players on a football team. The result is a work that grabs you and your toddler, and still gets the point across about numbers.

Hush! A Thai Lullaby *By Mingfong Ho and Holly Meade (illustration)*
It's bedtime, but all of the animals refuse to keep quiet, so it's time for mother to go to each of the animals and ask them to hush so baby can go to sleep. She goes to the frog, she goes to the elephant, she even goes to the mosquito, until all is quiet. In the end, everyone is asleep, with the noticeable exception of baby!

I Am Me! *By Alexa Brandenberg*

Brandenberg has put together a very clever book, playing off the "What do you want to be when you grow up?" question, by showing all sorts of girls and boys imagining that they are a fireman, a chef, a librarian, etc. All stereotypes are thrown to the wind in this great romp.

Just a Little Bit *By Ann Tompert and Lynn Munsinger (illustration)*

Going for a seesaw ride isn't supposed to be this much of a challenge, but when you have a mouse on one side of the seesaw and an elephant on the other, it takes some special assistance to be able to go up and down. Fortunately, the mouse and the elephant have a little help from their friends – the other animals. A great story that teaches some complex concepts.

Maisy's Colors *By Lucy Cousins*

Maisy is always a delight, and in this extra-large board book, she's out to teach your toddler colors. Readers have to look to find the featured color on the page, which is a great way to strengthen the recognition of color concepts.

Max's Bedtime *By Rosemary Wells*

How is Max to sleep now that he can't find his elephant? Ruby, his sister, thinks she knows the answer. She gives Max her bear, and then she gives him just about everything else. Finally, the pile on Max's bed grows so high that there's not any room left for Max, and he falls out of bed – right next to his elephant!

More More More Said the Baby: 3 Love Stories *By Vera Williams*

This is the ultimate in toddler love stories. What could be better than stories of babies running, giggling and being lifted into the arms of adults who hug, kiss and tuck them in to bed? The stylish watercolor drawings make this book well deserving of the Caldecott honor that it has received. A perfect bedtime story.

Mouse Mess *By Linnea Riley*

So it's bedtime for the human family? It's the perfect time for our hero, the mouse, to come in for his nightly snack in the kitchen. But our mouse does more than have a snack – he makes a mess as he builds castles from sugar and jumps into the corn flakes. The cut-paper collages set against the dark backgrounds are striking.

Mysterious Thelonious *By Chris Raschka*

This book, inspired by a work by Thelonious Monk, lets readers match colors to notes on a musical scale. A very clever introduction to music.

No, David! *By David Shannon*

David is a five-year-old boy, and no matter what he does, it turns out to be something he shouldn't be doing. David's mother is constantly reminding him of the things he shouldn't be doing, with the refrain, "No, David!" A great story about what it's like to be a child – and what it's like to be a parent.

O is for Orca: A Pacific Northwest Alphabet Book *By Andrea Helman and Art Wolfe (illustration)*

With "Auklet" instead of "apple," this is not your typical alphabet book. It features photographs of objects from the Pacific Northwest and is a great way to expose toddlers to words, animals and concepts that they would not normally encounter.

The Old Man & His Door *By Gary Soto and Joe Cepeda (illustration)*

Was I supposed to take the pig (el puerco) to the barbecue? I thought you said to take it to the door (la puerta)! So goes this funny tale of an old man stumbling his way throughout the day. During the adventure, readers are introduced to a number of Spanish words and definitions.

Seven Candles for Kwanzaa *By Andrea Pinkney and Brian Pinkney (illustration)*

In straightforward and engaging language, Pinkney introduces the traditions and rituals associated with Kwanzaa in terms and images that will capture the imaginations of both toddlers and adults alike.

Ten Little Rabbits *By Virginia Grossman and Sylvia Long (illustration)*

Grossman has masterfully connected a simple counting book with a story of Native American culture. The 10 little rabbits in the book hunt and trap and send smoke signals across to neighboring tribes. The charming words and illustrations earned this title *Parent Magazine's* "Book of the Year" award.

This is Me *By Lenore Blegvad and Erik Blegvad (illustration)*

As morning comes, a dawn of discovery begins. This story follows a toddler through his day, as he introduces himself to all of the things that are important to him – his bear, his clothes, his blocks and the parts of his body. As toddlers begin to develop a strong sense of themselves, this is a very nice book to accompany them on their journey.

Twist With a Burger, Jitter With a Bug *By Linda Lowery and Pat Dypold (illustration)*
The rhyme in this story jumps, bounces and bops in celebration of all types of dancing. Colorful background collages add to the whole spirit of movement and motion.

What's for Lunch: A Play-and-Read Book *By Eric Carle*
Eric Carle is one of the most prolific and beloved of all children's authors. In this book, Carle creates a monkey that is left in charge of 10 pieces of fruit. The monkey ends up making a very nice lunch of the fruit, as well as a nice lesson in numbers up to 10.

What the Sun Sees, What the Moon Sees *By Nancy Tafuri*
Reading the book in the "daylight" direction gives you street scenes, playgrounds and barnyards – all as seen in the light of day. Turn the book over, however, and you see the world in darkness. A great concept book for young children.

Who Hops *By Katie Davis*
A hilarious way to reinforce what animals do – by getting it wrong first, and then getting it right. Clean, bright, amusing graphics (a hippo sprouts little pink wings in an attempt to fly) make the game a favorite.

Zin! Zin! Zin! A Violin *By Lloyd Moss and Marjorie Priceman (illustration)*
This book combines a bit of everything – music, counting, colors, dance, poetry, instruments – and meshes them together to produce a beautiful book that engrosses children of all ages. The illustrations are brilliant and engaging.

"The self is not something ready-made, but something in continuous formation through choice of action."
JOHN DEWEY, PHILOSOPHER AND EDUCATOR

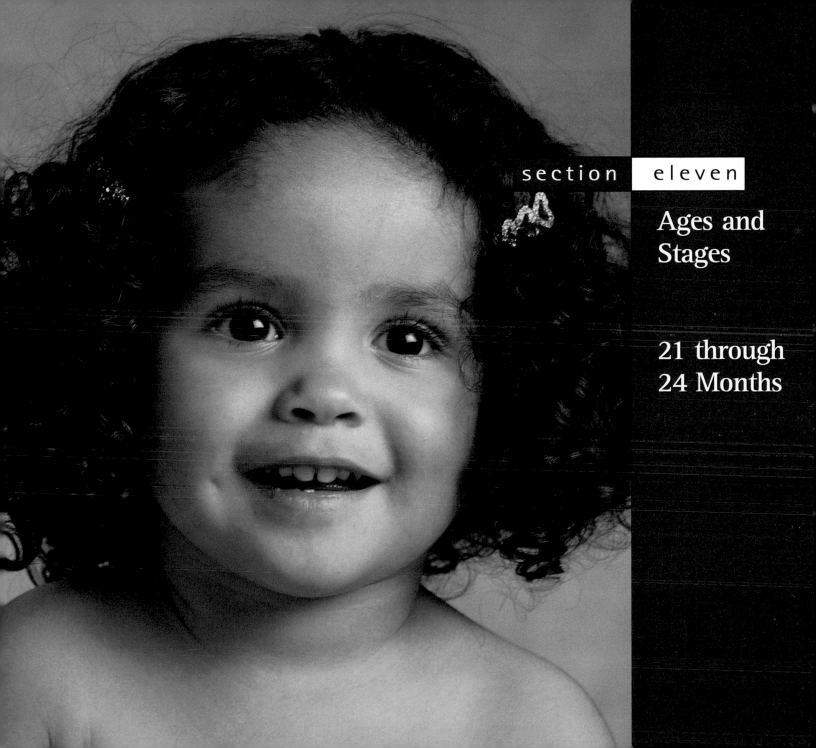

Ages and
Stages

21 through
24 Months

Ages and
Stages

21 through
24 Months

"Too often we underestimate the power of a touch,
a smile, a kind word, a listening ear,
an honest compliment, or the smallest act of caring,
all of which have the potential to turn a life around."

LEO BUSCAGLIA, PSYCHOANALYST

What You'll Discover In This Section

- What's Happening: 21 through 24 Months.

- Activities to Nurture Intellectual Development.

- Activities to Encourage Language Development.

- Activities to Nurture a Love of Music.

- Activities for Psycho-Motor Development.

- Activities for Social-Emotional Development.

- Books to Add to Your Library.

139

"Experience is never limited, and it is never complete; it is an immense sensibility, a kind of huge spider-web of the finest silken threads suspended in the chamber of consciousness and catching every air-borne particle in its tissue."

HENRY JAMES, AUTHOR

During this stage, your toddler adds a sense of imagination and creativity to her behavior. She becomes a true problem solver, with an improving ability to predict the potential outcomes of complex behaviors in which she might engage. Combining this understanding with improvements in her recognition memory enables her to efficiently manage her surroundings, which means less tripping on furniture and less time spent figuring out how to get the toy chest open. Trial-and-error behaviors, though always a part of learning, become less random; she spends more and more of her time planning out her activities.

Vocabulary growth continues with the addition of more and more two- and possibly three-word sentences. She may be able to give a full-blown description of what dad does to get ready for work. She also develops the ability to use a single word in multiple contexts – such as the tongue in her mouth and the tongue in her tennis shoes.

Further, as she encounters more and more objects, there is a great tendency to over-extend the use of labels to the wrong, but related objects – such as calling a stool a chair.

By the end of the second year, toddlers are able to incorporate words for theoretical concepts in their speech, even though they might not understand their meaning. She may, for example, talk about someone being "mean" to her but she may not have any idea what this means. One very nice result of the ability to think in the abstract is that your toddler begins to be able to label her emotional states, and in many instances, this ability enables her to communicate her emotions with words rather than actions. Between 18 and 24 months, divergence in word production by boys and girls becomes noticeable, as girls tend to produce a slightly higher number of words than do boys.

Although the negativism continues, for many parents and toddlers, a sense of balance begins to be established. Much to the delight of parents, toddlers in this age range are often very happy, smiling and laughing, and they can be very empathetic if someone else is in distress. However, it is not difficult for them to slip into fits of frustration or become quite demanding. One great development, related to advances in intellectual abilities, is that she can now use transitional objects, such as stuffed animals and blankets, as a source of comfort.

By age two, toddlers have become successful at so many things, that they now begin to expect to be successful; hence, you'll often see a toddler taking on tasks even well beyond her capabilities, such as climbing up the highchair now that she can climb up the stairs. With these expectations come appropriate emotional reactions, such as guilt at breaking a plate she tried to carry to pride at figuring out how to use a sippy cup to frustration at not being able to open the jelly jar.

Many toddlers at this age can reliably refer to themselves as girls or boys. As gender identification becomes important, you'll often find your toddler focusing on body parts of girls and boys; keep in mind that toddlers love to group things, and body parts – particularly boy body parts – are an obvious cue to group the sexes.

The silent dance we saw taking place between toddlers begins to become more of a fox trot. The interactions in which toddlers engage become more complex, with toddlers taking turns and specifying certain rules of the games they create. This play is not often well coordinated or long lasting, and as a result is not necessarily rewarding for the toddlers.

As your toddler's balance and strength continue to improve, she'll love to run, leap, climb and roll. It's a good idea to provide opportunities for acrobatics and climbing, being sure that all these activities are done in a safe place where they can be easily monitored.

From a fine motor standpoint, your toddler's ability to manipulate writing instruments such as crayons and pencils, improves markedly. Toddlers love to scribble and paint, and appreciate any opportunities you give them to do it. It can be fun to give them a simple geometric design to copy or draw them a house to fill in, but at this point, the name of the game is scribbling.

Parents tell it like it is:

"Alex has become very close to our neighbor's baby Joey. The other day, Joey was over for a visit, and started to cry. As soon as he heard Joey in distress, Alex grabbed Joey's bottle, ran over to him and proceeded to feed him until he quieted down."
JAY CYWAN, FATHER OF ALEX

Perception & Cognition	Vocalizations & Language	Social–Emotional	Motor
• Assembles and disassembles objects for fun. • Becomes increasingly aware of sounds, and increasingly fond of the repetition of these sounds, *e.g.*, hearing a song or a book over and over again. • Begins to want to choose things for herself, *e.g.*, bananas, yes; carrots, no. • Begins to understand the sequential order of events. • Begins to use reasoning, rather than trial-and-error, to solve problems. • Begins to be able to focus on a single task, while still being able to monitor other things happening in her environment. • Routines become an important tool in her ability to predict and be comfortable in her environment. • Begins to understand that she is a girl (or he a boy). • Begins to hum and sing songs with which she is familiar.	• Begins to refer to herself using her name. • Begins to use "I" and "me." • With the onset of multiple-word sentences, begins to use grammatical forms, *e.g.*, "Will you play with me?" • Begins to use the appropriate form of irregular verbs, *e.g.*, "thought" instead of "thinked" or "thunk." • Begins to combine words into two- and possibly three-word sentences. • Uses the terms "please" and "thank you" when prompted. • Begins to hold self-dialogues that reflect events in her daily life.	• Begins to assert her independence, *e.g.*, begins to favor the word "no." • Demonstrates pride in her accomplishments. • Becomes focused on possession of objects, *i.g.*, "that's mine." • Begins to engage in shared play with other toddlers. • Emotional states are longer lasting, and there is less rapid change between emotions. • Begins to become more sociable, and less confrontational and defiant. • Transitional objects become a source of comfort.	• Is able to stack up to four blocks. • Loves to test physical limits, *e.g.*, jumps off stairs or steps. • Is able to kick a large ball. • Begins to be able to push a pedal on a tricycle. • Is able to roughly copy a circle. • Begins to be able to manipulate puzzle pieces without handles. • Ability to reach for and grasp objects improves dramatically. • Begins to be able to jump short distances. • Is now able to play while squatting.

ACTIVITIES FOR BABIES FROM 21 THROUGH 24 MONTHS
ACTIVITIES TO NURTURE INTELLECTUAL DEVELOPMENT

Activity	Description of the Activity	Benefit
An Apple a Day ·	Cut an apple in half and closely examine the details. Talk about what the stem is for, discuss how the seeds are apple trees in the waiting and explain why we don't eat the core.	An exercise in observation, exploration and vocabulary development.
Two by Two	Go searching your house for things that come in pairs (candlesticks, lamps, speakers, etc.) Count them (one, two) as you go and count how many you find in total.	Teaches categorization and counting skills.
Baths: By the Numbers	As you prepare your toddler to take a bath, narrate the steps that you are going through — getting the water the correct temperature, filling the tub, taking off clothes, stepping in carefully, washing face, washing hair, drying off, putting on pajamas, etc.	A comforting ritual that strengthens sequencing skills.
Bouncing Cereal	Drop a few pieces of cereal into a small plastic bottle and ask your toddler to get them out. If she has any trouble, or is experiencing any frustration, help her, and then encourage her to do it on her own next time.	Demonstrates cause-and-effect relationships and exercises problem-solving and creative thinking skills.
Butterfly Inkblots	Using watercolor paints and construction paper, make 'Butterfly Inkblots!' Paint one side of the paper, then fold it over to make a butterfly. Cut the butterflies out when they're dry, and fly them around the room.	Creative play that teaches color understanding, develops fine motor skills and inspires imaginative play.
Hang It Up	Hang a short clothesline between the backs of two chairs. Using clothespins, hang pictures, objects or colored pieces of paper — anything — to make a simple pattern. Help her continue the pattern on her own. Closely monitor, and properly dispose of the clothesline when you are finished.	Teaches color concepts, patterning and fine motor skills — while providing practice with symbols.
Dominoes	Place two large dominoes on the table, being sure that the two dominoes share a number on one side. Ask your toddler which two sides should go together. As she masters this skill, move up to three dominoes.	Teaches pattern recognition and pre-counting skills.

Activity	Description of the Activity	Benefit
Feely Box	Cut a hole in the top of a shoe box, large enough to fit your child's hand. Place different items in the shoe box, one at a time, making sure that the items vary in texture (*e.g.*, a piece of silk, an emery board, a small bean bag). Place a matching set of items outside of the box. Have your toddler reach in and feel an object, and then, without taking the item out of the box, select the item on the outside of the box that matches the one on the inside. Open the box up if she's right.	Exercises fine motor skills, psycho-motor development and memory.
Grocery List	Create a picture grocery list. As you walk through the aisles of the market, let your toddler hold the list and point out the items on the shelf.	Builds pre-literacy skills, develops fine motor skills and provides practice in linking objects and symbols.
Growing Pictures	On a single piece of construction paper, cut out one large circle, one medium circle and one small circle. Set the shapes aside — it's the holes you'll be using. Choose a picture of an object that your toddler knows well — such as a face — and place the small circular hole over the picture. See if she can recognize the picture. If not, move to the medium sized hole and finally the large sized hole. Eventually remove the paper and show her the whole picture.	Strengthens recognition and memory skills, and teaches size and shape concepts.
Hard and Soft Boiled	During clean up time, start by picking up things that have hard surfaces, and then those that have soft surfaces. Have your toddler carry a sack for the soft, you take one for the hard. When the sacks become too heavy to carry, go put everything away.	Develops gross motor and categorization skills, and provides a unique tactile experience.
I'm Taller Than That!	Stroll around the house and look for things that are taller, shorter or the same size as your toddler. Carrying around a yardstick is a concrete way of showing the difference.	Develops fine motor and pre-math skills.
Submarines	When your toddler is in the bathtub, place a large plastic bottle in the tub. Do the same with a smaller plastic bottle, and watch how they slowly fill up with water, and eventually sink.	Demonstrates cause-and-effect relationships and teaches pre-math concepts.

Activity	Description of the Activity	Benefit
Mighty Megaphone	Take an empty paper towel roll, and use it as a megaphone. Announce a show or a special event, then let your toddler have a turn. Talk about how your voice changes when you use the megaphone.	A lesson in cause-and-effect relationships that develops gross motor skills and inspires imaginative play.
The Container Test	Take a selection of plastic storage containers and lids. Sit down and help your toddler match the lids to the containers. As her fine motor skills improve, show her how to take the lids off, and then replace them again.	Strengthens perceptual, memory and reasoning skills and later, fine motor skills.
Rain, Rain, Go Away	After a fresh rain, take a walk in your garden. Look at how the water sticks on some plants, flows off others, sinks into the ground in some spots and creates puddles in others.	A lesson in cause-and-effect relationships.
Spoons Here, Forks There	As you take the silverware from the sink or dishwasher, have your toddler help put away the spoons and forks. Try counting the number of tablespoons you've put away. Are there more of those than salad forks?	Develops categorization skills, counting skills, more than/less than relationships and fine motor skills.
Starched Strips	Tear strips of thin paper, and dip them into a mixture of cornstarch and water; add food coloring, if you'd like. Help your toddler wrap the strips on plastic bottles or other non-breakable items to create three-dimensional art.	Exercises fine motor skills and creativity.
Sorting Groceries	As you unpack your groceries, let your toddler put away light, non-breakable items. Let her tell you where she thinks they go. Do the crackers go in the refrigerator? Does the pasta go in the flour bin?	Teaches categorization and fine motor skills, strengthens memory and encourages social skills.
The Menu Spinner	Cut out a circular "spinner" from some colorful construction paper. Punch a hole in the middle of a paper plate and in the middle of the spinner. Attach the spinner to the plate with a brass fastener. Glue pictures of some of your toddler's favorite foods to the paper plate. At mealtime, let her move the spinner to the picture of the food she would like.	Develops fine motor skills, teaches color concepts and provides practice in linking objects and symbols.

Activity	Description of the Activity	Benefit
The Guessing Game	Use two empty shoe boxes and a favorite stuffed animal to play "The Guessing Game." Hide the animal in one of the boxes and let your toddler guess which box hides the toy. Move the boxes around to try and trick her. As she gets good at this, add a third box.	Develops an understanding of object permanence and builds memory skills.
The Shredding Machine	Cut the top page of a spiral notebook into wide strips. On the page underneath, tape a picture that is very familiar to your toddler—such as a familiar face. One by one, lift the strips until enough of the image is showing for her to recognize it. Try varying the shape and width of the strips that you cut.	Builds pre-literacy skills, strengthens recognition memory and provides practice with symbols.
Chef for the Day	Lay out all the ingredients you need to make a sandwich, and let your toddler be the chef. Even if she can't spread the mustard, she can tell you that it's time to do it.	A lesson in sequential order that develops fine motor skills and builds confidence.
Which One Has More?	Fill one short vase with colored water. Fill a second, taller vase so that the liquid is at the same level as the first vase. Ask your toddler if one vase has more liquid in it than the other, then test her answer in two identically shaped bowls.	Teaches size, shape and color concepts and builds pre-math skills.
Shape Sorting	Cut triangles, circles and squares from construction paper. Make sure some are big and some are small, some are red, some are yellow and some are blue. Show her how you can separate out the squares by putting them in one pile, the triangles in another and the circles in a third. Let her try it. Once she has this down, show her how you can sort them by their color, or their size, too.	Teaches size, shape, color and grouping concepts.
Water Art	Grab a small bucket of water and some tennis balls, and take a seat in your driveway. Dunk a ball in the water and roll it either up or down to make a line or an arc. Talk about the words "uphill" and "downhill." Take a walk along all the trails the water left behind.	Demonstrates cause-and-effect relationships and teaches size and shape concepts.

Activity	Description of the Activity	Benefit
Baked Names	Whip up a batch of bread dough, or purchase frozen dough at the market. Use alphabet cookie cutters, or a knife, to make the letters of your child's name. Bake, and don't forget to eat them.	Builds pre-literacy skills and provides practice in sequential events.
Going on a Square Hunt	Go for a walk in your neighborhood, hunting for squares (or triangles or rectangles.) Look high and low and all around. Count how many you find.	Builds language development and perception skills and teaches size and shape concepts.
Hop In, Hop Out	Draw a circle on the sidewalk with chalk. Have your toddler stand inside the circle, while you are on the outside. Talk about being "in" and being "out." Now, switch positions by jumping over the line.	Fosters language learning, teaches size and shape and inside and outside concepts.
It's Magnifying	Pick some flowers from the garden and arrange them in a vase. Now, take out a magnifying glass and study them up close.	Develops an understanding of perception, teaches color concepts and exercises categorization skills.
Tag: With a Base	Play tag with your toddler, and make a safe base on the couch. Whenever someone gets tagged, change the safe place to somewhere new and unusual. Name the safe base.	Exercises gross motor skills, teaches new vocabulary and encourages social skills.
Tell Me What Happened Today	Choose a special time to talk about your day — such as dinner or bedtime. Tell your toddler what you did during the day. As she gets older, ask her what she did, and help her to remember.	Builds language skills and family unity, strengthens memory and develops social skills.
What's My Name?	Arrange a set of magnetic letters on the refrigerator. Every morning after breakfast, spell a new word. Start with her name, then do the pet's name, sister's name, etc.	Strengthens pre-literacy skills and provides practice with symbols.
Tie A Yellow Ribbon	Walk around the yard with your toddler and tie a blue ribbon to the jasmine bush, a green ribbon to the hydrangea and a yellow ribbon to the old oak tree. Now run from ribbon to ribbon saying, "Let's run to the jasmine — that's the blue one." As she begins to learn the names of the plants, remove the ribbons and add more plants.	Develops muscles, vocabulary and memory and teaches color concepts.

Activity	Description of the Activity	Benefit
Where it Stops, Nobody Knows	Tape a group of similar pictures (such as a group of animals) to a Lazy Susan. Give the spinner a good push, and ask your toddler to guess what picture landed in front of her. Is it the horse? The pig? Name the animal, make the sound the animal makes and talk about where the animal lives.	Introduces new concepts and new words, provides practice with symbols and strengthens memory.
You've Got Mail	Encourage family members and friends to send mail to your toddler, and occasionally slip something in yourself. Celebrate its arrival, and sit together and read the details. Don't be afraid to send long letters—it just extends the joyful time that you get to sit and read together.	Promotes pro-social, language and pre-literacy skills.

ACTIVITIES TO NURTURE A LOVE OF MUSIC

Activity	Description of the Activity	Benefit
A Ride to Bed	As part of a bedtime ritual, recite this rhyme and follow the associated actions: *Ride on Daddy's knee dear* *And see what you can see dear* *The cows are in the clover* *The pigs have gone to Dover* *Ride on Daddy's back dear* *And give the whip a crack dear* *Around the table and dining chairs* *And then we'll ride to bed upstairs*	A comforting ritual that reinforces language development and musical awareness.
Gallant Ship	Holding your toddler's hands up high, walk in circles to the rhythm of the rhyme. On the final line of the verse, slowly slump to the floor: *Three times around went our gallant ship* *And three times around went she* *Three times around went our gallant ship* *And we sank to the bottom of the sea*	Reinforces language development and musical awareness, and strengthens both gross and fine motor skills.

Activity	Description of the Activity	Benefit
Hey! Ho! Anybody Home?	Recite the following rhyme with your toddler. Start by covering your toddler's eyes, and at the question, "Anybody Home?" remove your hands, and give your toddler a kiss. At the "tapped," and "knock, knock" lines, gently tap on the floor: *Hey! Ho! Anybody home?* *I've tapped at your windows* *And knocked at your door* *Tell me, tell me,* *Where can you be?* *Hey! Ho! Anybody home?* *Knock! Knock!*	Reinforces language development, musical awareness and fine motor skills.
Let's Chase the Squirrel	Sit on the floor facing your toddler. Recite the rhyme, and at the end, you both stand up, and you try to tag her. Take turns doing the chasing: *Let us chase the squirrel* *Up the hickory, down the hickory* *Let us chase the squirrel* *Up the hickory tree*	Reinforces language development and strengthens both gross motor skills and overall balance.
Oh, Little Birdie	Recite the following rhyme whenever you see a bird: *Oh little birdie,* *You're getting wet on your head* *You better go to bed* *Oh little birdie* *Your mommy loves you* *She says, "Come home, too!"*	A comforting social ritual that reinforces language development and musical awareness.

Activity	Description of the Activity	Benefit
No More Pie	Sit on the floor with your toddler facing you. Repeat the rhyme together: *Oh my* *No more pie* *I want a piece of meat* *Meat's too red* *I want a piece of bread* *Bread's too brown* *I think I'll go to town* *Town's too far* *I think I'll take a car* *Car won't go* *I fell and stubbed my toe* *Toe gives me pain* *I think I'll take a train* *Train had a wreck* *I fell and hurt my neck* *Oh my* *No more pie*	Reinforces language development and musical awareness.
Old John the Rabbit	Sit on the floor with your toddler and recite the following rhyme. On each of the words (except "oh, yes"), tap the ground. Repeat the verse as many times as you like and add more vegetables: *Old John the rabbit, oh, yes!* *Old John the rabbit, oh, yes!* *Had a very bad habit, oh, yes!* *Of going to my garden, oh, yes!* *And eating up my peas, oh, yes!* *And eating my tomatoes, oh, yes!* *And...*	Reinforces language development, musical awareness and fine motor skills.

Activity	Description of the Activity	Benefit
One Little Duck	Sit on the floor with your toddler and recite the following rhyme. Sometimes say the "Quack! Quack! Quack!" loudly, other times say it softly. On the last verse, change the "did not come back" line to "That little duck came running back!" *One little duck went out to play* *Over the hill and far away* *But the mommy duck said* *Quack! Quack! Quack!* *That little duck did not come back!*	Reinforces language development, musical awareness and voice control.
Pop! Goes the Weasel	As you sing this song with your toddler, gently rub her hands together. At the word "Pop!" clap her hands together, then throw her arms wide open: *All around the carpenter's bench,* *The monkey chased the weasel* *The monkey thought it was all in fun* *Pop! Goes the weasel*	Reinforces language development, musical awareness and fine motor skills.
Ride a Cock Horse	Sit on the floor with your knees bent and place your toddler on your thighs, facing away from you. As you recite the rhyme, bounce your knees as if she is riding a horse: *Ride a cock-horse to Banbury Cross* *To see a kind lady, up on a white horse* *Rings on her fingers and bells on her toes* *She shall have music wherever she goes*	Reinforces language development, musical awareness and gross motor skills.

Activity	Description of the Activity	Benefit
Shoe a Little Horse	Sit on the floor with your toddler facing away from you. Remove her shoes and socks. Recite the following rhyme, and as you do so, gently tap her feet to the rhythm of the beat: *Shoe a little horse* *Shoe a little mare* *But let the little colt* *Go bare, bare, bare*	Reinforces language development, musical awareness and body awareness.
The Little Mice	Sit with your toddler on your lap, facing you. As you recite this rhyme, hold her hand in yours, and with your index finger, make gentle circles in her hand. On the word "house," run your fingers up over her arm and tickle her under her arm: *The little mice go creeping, creeping, creeping* *The little mice go creeping* *All through the house*	Reinforces language development, musical awareness and body awareness.
This Little Cow Eats Grass	Sit in a chair with your toddler facing you on your lap. Take her hand in yours and softly recite this rhyme. Starting with the first line, gently hold your toddler's thumb between your thumb and forefinger. With each subsequent verse, move to the next finger on your toddler's hand. On the final line, just run your fingers all the way up to your toddler's chin and tickle her: *This little cow eats grass* *This little cow eats hay* *This little cow drinks water* *This little cow runs away* *And this little cow does nothing but just lies all day* *We'll chase her, we'll chase her, we'll chase her away*	Reinforces language development, musical awareness and body awareness.

Activity	Description of the Activity	Benefit
Two Little Eyes	Sit in a chair and situate your toddler so that she is facing you in your lap. As you recite the rhyme, gently touch her eyes, then ears, nose and finally her mouth: *Two little eyes to look around* *Two little ears to hear each sound* *One little nose to smell what's sweet* *One little mouth that likes to eat*	Reinforces language development and musical- and self-awareness.
What's My Instrument?	Sit on the floor and show your toddler three instruments: ones that make dramatically different sounds work best, such as a triangle, a drum and a recorder. Have your child close her eyes, and then play one of the instruments. Have her open her eyes, and pick which one you played.	Demonstrates cause-and-effect relationships, introduces the timbre of various instruments and exercises memory skills.

ACTIVITIES FOR PSYCHO-MOTOR DEVELOPMENT

Activity	Description of the Activity	Benefit
Bend and Stretch	Push aside the furniture for some bending and stretching. Let your toddler mimic you as you reach for the sky, rotate your ankles and do a few stomach crunches. Be careful not to overdo these exercises.	Promotes strength, balance and coordination, and inspires imitative play.
Balancing Bean Bags	Have your toddler balance a small bean bag on the top of her outstretched hand. Start with her right hand, then move to the left. As she gets better, have her balance it on the top of her foot, with her foot slightly elevated.	Strengthens fine and gross motor skills.
Basting	Next time she's taking a bath, give your toddler a large turkey baster, and show her how to squeeze it to suck up the water. Next, show her how to squeeze the water out.	Strengthens major arm muscles and demonstrates cause-and-effect relationships.

Activity	Description of the Activity	Benefit
Ping Pong Ball Submarine	Next time she's in the bath, give her a ball that floats and have her try to hold it under the water.	Exercises both fine and gross motor skills.
Fast Circle Slow	Hold your toddler's hands and walk in circles. Start fast, then go slow. Do this to music and vary the pace to the beat.	Exercises fine and gross motor skills and develops overall balance.
From This Bowl to That	Fill one medium-sized bowl with water and a bit of water-based paint. Leave a second bowl empty. Show your toddler how to use a measuring cup to scoop up the colored liquid from the first bowl and transfer it into the second.	Strengthens both coordination and fine motor skills, and teaches pre-math and color concepts.
Gone Fishing II	Tie a magnet to one end of a string, and a stick to the other end for your toddler to hold. Place metal bottle tops, paper clips or small metal toys in the bottom of a box, then, let the fishing expedition begin. Monitor closely and properly dispose of the string when you are finished.	Exercises fine motor skills, teaches cause-and-effect relationships and inspires imaginative play.
Haul the Haul	Place three small objects, such as blocks or balls, on the floor and demonstrate how you can carry all three by holding one in each hand, and balancing the last between your arm and your belly. Encourage her to do the same.	Exercises coordination skills and teaches size, shape and counting concepts.
Pigs in a Blanket	Hold one side of your toddler's blanket and show her how to hold the other. Place one of her favorite stuffed animals in the middle, and try to roll the animal back and forth. Next, try to make the animal bounce, but remain on the blanket. Finally, toss the stuffed animal as high as you can.	Exercises fine and gross motor skills.
Rake the Leaves	While you're raking the leaves, give her a toy rake so she can help. When you've made a big pile, jump in!	Exercises fine motor skills and inspires imitative play.

Activity	Description of the Activity	Benefit
Roll Left, Roll Right	Find a grassy hill with a very mild slope. Roll down together on your right sides. Climb the hill, and do it all over again, but this time, roll down on your left sides.	Exercises both sides of the body and teaches body awareness.
Shake Your Hands ...	To the melody of "Row, Row, Row Your Boat," sing the following and act out the hand motions of each verse, then add some of your own. *Shake, Shake, Shake Your Hands* *Roll, Roll, Roll Your Fists* *Wiggle, Wiggle, Wiggle Your Fingers ...*	Exercises fine motor skills and reinforces the understanding of melody.
Soccer: Part II	Practice kicking a large beach ball back and forth with your toddler. As this skill is mastered, create a goal by placing two chairs approximately five feet apart from each other, and let her practice kicking the ball through the goal. As her skills improve, have her move a few feet back from the goal and/or move the chairs closer together.	Exercises muscles, overall balance and fine motor skills while building confidence.
Splitting Hairs	Cook spaghetti, let it cool, then let your toddler play with the long strands. Show her how to line them up, or curl one in circles.	Strengthens fine motor skills, teaches concepts of size and shape and provides a great tactile experience.
The Nose Test	Cut a lemon and an orange and douse a piece of paper with vanilla or any other identifiable fragrance. Show them to your toddler. Now place a blindfold over her eyes. Ask your toddler to smell each smell, then name the object that she's smelling.	Fosters language learning and strengthens memory skills.
The Bubble Stomp	Blow bubbles and let your toddler clap them into oblivion. Next let her try stomping on them.	Demonstrates cause-and-effect relationships, builds balance, and develops fine and gross motor skills.

ACTIVITIES FOR BABIES FROM 21 THROUGH 24 MONTHS
ACTIVITIES FOR PSYCHO-MOTOR DEVELOPMENT (CONTINUED)

Activity	Description of the Activity	Benefit
The Chase	Play a game of chase. Make sure you are on a soft, carpeted or grassy surface, get down on all fours (it's not quite as scary that way) and go get her. Take turns, and let her chase you.	Develops gross motor skills and inspires imaginative and imitative play.
The Sidestep	Play a game of match me. Walk sideways, in circles, or backward, and encourage her to follow your lead. Trade places, and now you follow her.	Develops gross motor skills and inspires imitative play.

ACTIVITIES FOR SOCIAL EMOTIONAL DEVELOPMENT

Activity	Description of the Activity	Benefit
Dusting Mittens	Let your toddler wear an old pair of mittens and use them to help you dust.	Develops self-awareness and pro-social behavior.
Daily Walk	Create a daily walk ritual. Go at approximately the same time each day and go on the same route. Point out landmarks as you go and look for things that have changed — such as trees, gardens, the color of someone's house, etc.	A comforting social ritual that exercises memory skills and muscle coordination.
All the World's a Stage	Act out one of your favorite stories. Let your toddler be whichever character she chooses, and you be all the rest. Use costumes and props as appropriate.	Teaches understanding of other people's motivations and intentions, and inspires imaginative and imitative play.
Long Distance Reading	If you or your spouse will be away for an evening, record yourself reading one of your toddler's favorite books. At storytime, instruct whoever's home to play the recording.	A comforting ritual that reinforces a love of reading.
Swim Doll, Swim	Fill a sink or tub with water. Have your toddler teach a favorite rubber doll how to "swim" by moving the doll's arms and feet through the water.	Develops body and self-awareness, and inspires imaginative and imitative play.
Walk a Mile in My Shoes	If your spouse is at work, or a sibling is at school, spend some time during the day talking with your toddler about what they may be doing.	Teaches an understanding of the motivations, intentions and actions of other people.

Books to Add to Your 21- through 24-Month-Old's Library

Alphababies *By Kim Golding*
This book is an odd combination of things – really cute babies merged with computer graphics for costumes and backgrounds, letters everywhere and a matching rhyme to go with it. This is a busy book, but we know that babies love to look at babies, the catchy rhymes will help foster language development and bright backgrounds will catch your toddler's attention.

Angela's Wings *By Eric Jon Nones*
This is a parable about a girl named Angela, who must deal with her friends and family when she suddenly sprouts wings. Her first reaction is to hope no one will notice; her second, embarrassment. But all this changes when her grandmother helps point out how unique all of us are, and how wings are a special gift.

Annie's Gifts *By Angela Medearis and Anna Rich (illustration)*
Sometimes it's tough growing up in a family where brothers and sisters have special talents. Annie happens to be growing up in a family where both her brother and sister have great musical talent, but when Annie plays, let's just say she doesn't make beautiful music. Annie eventually finds her own special talents in her ability to draw and write.

Carolina Shout! *By Alan Schroeder and Bernie Fuchs (illustration)*
For Delia, Charleston, South Carolina in the years before World War II is alive with music. Music is everywhere – in the raindrops and in the call of the frogs. A lovely book about listening.

The Chanukkah Guest *By Eric Kimmel and Giora Carmi (illustration)*
It's not always the easiest thing to introduce children to the intricacies of a holiday like Chanukkah, but throw in a bear and a loving bubba (Yiddish for grandmother) who makes the best latkes (potato pancakes) in the world and you can pull it off. Bubba Brayna, mistakes a bear for a rabbi, and ends up entertaining the entire village.

Chidi Only Likes Blue: An African Book of Colors *By Ifeoma Onyefulu*
A tale of how colors work, set in the Nigerian culture and complemented by beautiful photographs. Chidi tells his sister, Nneka, that he only likes blue. Nneka sets out to show her brother that there are many reasons to like other colors besides his beloved blue.

Children Just Like Me: In Association with UNICEF
By Susan Copsey and Barnabas Kindersley (illustration)
Children come in all shapes and sizes, from all parts of the world, and as different as we all are, we're not as different as we might think. This walk through the lives of children is a beautiful introduction to cultural diversity.

Exactly the Opposite *By Tana Hoban*
This book is filled with colorful photographs of paired objects – all opposites. Even without words, this book does a fabulous job of getting across the concept of opposites.

Fiesta! *By Ginger Guy and Rene Moreno (illustration)*
Go on a shopping expedition through the aisles of a mercado (market), and pick up the things you need. This is an English/Spanish bilingual counting book, complete with large and catchy illustrations.

Flossie and the Fox *By Patricia McKissack and Rachel Isadora (illustration)*
Mama sends Flossie Finley off on an errand and warns her about that sly fox who's been out stealing eggs. When Flossie meets the fox, she's not sure what to do, because she's never seen a fox before. Flossie's attempt to get the fox to prove his identity makes for a delightful tale.

Hunterman and the Crocodile: A West African Folktale
By Baba Diakité
This elegantly illustrated story comes from a traditional West African Folktale. In this parable of the relationship between man and nature, a hunter must deal with crocodiles that have a mind of their own.

If You Give a Pig a Pancake *By Laura Numeroff and Felicia Bond (illustration)*
If your toddler loves either of the first two books in this series – "If You Give a Mouse a Cookie" and "If You Give a Moose a Muffin" – treat yourself to this new book. It's the same story with the same point, but with a pig in the leading role.

King Bidgood's in the Bathtub *By Audrey Wood and Don Wood (illustration)*

The king is in the bathtub and he refuses to come out. The queen can't get him to come out. The prince can't get him to come out. All the members of the court can't get him to come out. Finally, a very clever pig outsmarts them all and rescues the kingdom.

The Little Blue and Little Yellow *By Leo Lionni*

Leo Lionni is the recipient of four individual Caldecott Honor awards, for his books "Inch by Inch," "Frederick," "Swimmy" and "Alexander and the Wind-Up Mouse." "Little Blue and Little Yellow" is actually Lionni's first work, and where the other titles mentioned are most appropriate for children over age four, this book is appropriate for very young children. It's a classic story of how friendship can bring people, or colors, together. When read as a parable, this story also has a wonderful message of racial harmony.

Max's Chocolate Chicken *By Rosemary Wells*

Max is a rather mischievous toddler (as he has shown in "Max's Dragon Shirt" and "Max's Christmas"). In this book, Max wants to gather the most Easter eggs so he can get the prize he covets – the chocolate chicken. But, as we all know, toddlers are easily distracted, and it's basically impossible for Max to beat his older sister, Ruby, in this task of wits. In the end, Max finds a way to overcome the odds in an amusing, if not perfectly acceptable way.

Moonbathing *By Liz Rosenberg and Stephen Lambert (illustration)*

The beach in the daytime is a magical experience, but at nighttime, it can be an almost mystical one. A young girl and her older cousin go on a trek on the beach at night, looking for buried treasure and meeting a friendly seal.

No Mirrors in My Nana's House *By Ysaye Barnwell and Synthia Saint James (illustration)*

This is a powerful book that passes along messages of love and self-esteem. The words are actually the chorus of a song and we highly recommend getting the version with the attached CD. They'll bring pleasure and entertainment for years to come.

The Relatives Came *By Cynthia Rylant and Stephen Gammel (illustration)*

This is a lively story of relative after relative coming for a visit and turning the house upside down. A fun story for the young children with big families.

Shortcut *By David Macaulay*

All seems rather straightforward when Albert sets off with his horse to the market. But throughout the course of nine stories, Albert learns how things go together, and what causes what. It's a great introduction to the whole concept of cause-and-effect.

Snow *By Uri Shulevitz*

Everyone says "no snow." The television report says "no snow." The radio report says "no snow." Much to the delight of one small boy and his dog, though, the snow does come. The excitement and energy of the new snow are wonderfully caught on these pages.

Snowflake Bentley *By Jacqueline Briggs and Mary Azarian (illustration)*

A Caldecott Winner, this story gives children a lovely retrospective look at rural America. The main character of the story is a boy named Wilson Bentley, who loved snow so much that he vows to grow up to be a photographer so that he can capture the beautiful world of snowflakes. The action takes place as farmers work their ox teams across a snowy landscape by the light of a lantern.

'Twas the Night B'Fore Christmas: An African-American Version *By Clement Moore and Melodye Rosales (illustration)*

This is a classic with a twist. The images are rich, and the turn-of-the-century approach to this story helps simultaneously highlight differences and similarities in cultural perspectives.

Welcoming Babies *By Margy Knight and Anne O'Brien (illustration)*

There is no more joyous event in all of the world than the birth of baby. This book shows the way people around the world celebrate this great event, with illustrations and text that invite readers of all ages into the celebrations.

Where's Chimpy *By Berniece Rabe and Diane Schmidt (illustration)*

On the surface this is a simple story – a father helping a little girl find one of her favorite stuffed animals. What makes this story just a little more special is the fact that the little girl has Down syndrome. Rabe has presented this fact without saying a word about it, making the story and the message one that will mature along with your toddler.

section twelve

Resources
& References

section twelve

Resources
& References

> *"Thought is the wind, knowledge the sail,*
>
> *and mankind the vessel."*
>
> AUGUST HARE, AUTHOR

What You'll Discover | In This Section

- Websites providing information on:
  - Clearinghouses that link you to other sites
  - Parenting Forums
  - Brain Development
  - Education
  - Children's Book Recommendations
  - Music
  - Giftedness
  - Assessment and Special Needs
  - Emergent Literacy
  - Health and Safety
- Books providing information on:
  - Brain/Intellectual Development
  - Social-Emotional Development
  - Literacy
  - Music

Websites and Organizations

Clearinghouses

Websites pointing you in the direction of more specific sites, although some of them have very good interactive capabilities themselves.

Baby Engine
www.novasight.com/babyeng/index.html
A great site that provides a search engine for looking up other baby-related websites. Each listing includes a summary so that parents can preview other web pages. Topics include parenting, education, medicine, literature, software, TV and movies. The chat room is easy to use and information posted seems particularly relevant for parents of very young children.

Babies Today
www.babiestoday.com
Dedicated to new parents this website includes an extensive resource section and nice practical links. Parents can find topics of special interest, such as pages dedicated to breastfeeding resources and "Mom's Health." Discussion forums and e-mail lists provide an easy way for parents to ask each other questions and share experiences. An expert is also available in the Q&A section to answer questions about safety, child development and medical topics. User-friendly and well-organized.

Children Now
www.childrennow.org
Most impressive about this site is its large links page, providing practical sites concerning health, education, safety, advocacy and government groups dedicated to children's welfare. Reports, action guides and complete documents are also available, discussing the most current happenings in the media. A monthly mailing list provides updates on federal legislation, action alerts and resources on children's issues both on and off the Internet. This is a good place to begin when searching for specialty topic groups.

ERIC
www.ericps.crc.uiuc.edu/eece/index.html
A clearinghouse for on elementary and early childhood education. Parents can find and focus on sites related to topics such as: assessment and evaluation, elementary and early childhood education, the National Parent Information Network and child care. Recommended sites provide a wealth of information related to each topic.

National Child Care Information Center
www.nccic.org
This website features a wide range of easily accessed child care topics. They provide useful links to other organizations and publications. Topics include a number of subjects such as brain development, child care for different age groups, health and literacy. Also provided are the directories for State agencies and organizations, complete with phone numbers and websites.

National Network for Child Care
www.exnet.iastate.edu/pages/families/nncc/homepage.html
Focuses on strengthening child care by linking the education, technology and research resources. This clearinghouse has pages relating to various childhood issues, including: health and safety, discipline, abuse, disabilities and activities and links to additional parenting sites. Article summaries come from various academic and research institutions and are full of helpful information and tips. Information also includes a series entitled, "Is your baby safe at home?" that parents can download. A great site!

STCs Education and Fun Page for Students, Teachers, Parents
http://home.earthlink.net/~stcarr/
Very large educational index with message boards and useful links for teachers, parents and children. The focus is on science, education and fun.

Teaching Strategies, Inc.
www.teachingstrategies.com
This is a good clearinghouse for links related to parental involvement in child education sites. Parent pages focus on what your child should be getting from a child care setting. The site creators discuss key developmental domains (*e.g.*, self, emotions).

Parenting Forums

These sites cover every imaginable parenting topic in forms ranging from open discussion forums to interactive magazines.

American Baby
www.americanbaby.com
The focus of this web magazine is support for new and expecting mothers. Mothers chat with other mothers with the same due date and review articles on breastfeeding, prenatal testing and using a birthing center. A great site!

Baby Center
www.babycenter.com
A rich site, where parents can get information on preconception, pregnancy or babies. Parents can plug in their child's age to get information on their baby's development. Other features include a chat room, question and answers with infant experts and checklists of things to do with an infant to encourage development, or questions to ask the pediatrician. Links to other useful sites are provided, and articles are cross-referenced with related topics.

Baby Talk
www.talkcity.com/calendar/category/parenting.html
This site is dedicated to discussion forums for parents and caregivers providing parents the opportunity to discuss issues between themselves, and with experts in the area of child development.

Baby Workshop
www.ctw.org/babyworkshop/
This site has been created by the people who bring you Sesame Street. Parents will find information on activities to share with their babies, a forum to share advice with other parents and a set of recommendations on where parents can go for additional information. A monthly newsletter is also available, providing parents customized information.

Babyworld
www.babyworld.co.uk/
A rich magazine from Great Britain that has a wealth of information on topics such as pregnancy, babies, young children, health, breastfeeding, screening, nutrition, behavior, development, growth, baby products, nurseries and equipment.

CyberMom Dot Com
www.thecybermom.com
A web magazine for moms, featuring chat forums and information articles. It's cute, user-friendly and provides helpful tips on dealing with everyday issues, such as step-parenting and eating. Parents can select a topic they are concerned about and find educational research-based information, additional book and web resources, organizations for support.

Early Childhood Educator
www.edpsych.com
People who teach young children will find new information, news, ideas and inspiration for parents, teachers and directors of programs for young children, all presented in a quick, easy-to-use format. Features include a free newsletter, tons of resource links, fresh articles, tips on parenting and teaching, and professional development materials and products.

Midlife Mommies
www.midlifemommies.com
A magazine website where older moms can find articles and tips on issues including tubal reversal, risks of later pregnancies, help with stepchildren, career advice and personal stories. Authors who post articles include their credentials (where applicable), addresses and e-mail.

Newborn's Page
www.kidsource.com:80/kidsource/pages/Newborns.html
Great selection of articles on newborn development, newborn safety and links to newborn websites. Whole articles are presented, sometimes with an extensive table of contents. Articles often include background information, further articles for review, relevant websites, personal stories, medical information websites and news/opinion stories.

ParentPartners
www.parentpartners.com
ParentPartners translates the latest developments in early learning theory and providing practical parenting advice and developmentally appropriate products and services for parents.

Single Rose
www.singlerose.com
A great website for single mothers — tips on getting child support, articles written specifically for single mothers, chat rooms and a profile of the single mother of the week. Single mothers might find this site a great source of support and encouragement.

The National Parenting Center (TNPC)
www.tnpc.com
Presented in a large magazine format with articles centering on parenting issues, including pregnancy, discipline and learning. Articles are written by physicians and pediatricians, and parents can focus on their child's specific age group (infant, toddler, preschool, school-aged, adolescent).

Brain Development

I Am Your Child Campaign
www.iamyourchild.org
Provides information about ages and stages, how early experience affects lifelong development and recent findings in brain research. Top experts in the field provide insights and tips on development. In addition, a list of television shows, books, magazines, videos and other reference materials is provided to parents.

Neuroscience for Kids
weber.u.washington.edu/~chudler/neurok.html
This site was created for students and teachers who are interested in learning about the nervous system. It has a surprising wealth of information, including activities and experiments to help parents and children learn about the brain.

Neurosciences on the Internet
www.dana.org
The Dana Alliance for Brain Initiatives is a nonprofit organization dedicated to advancing education on brain research through annual grants for continuing education. The foundation is associated with more than 170 preeminent neuroscientists, including six Nobel laureates. You will find a description of the foundation, the grant process and links to many other sites dealing specifically with brain development issues.

Neurosmith
www.neurosmith.com
Neurosmith's mission is to combine the latest brain research and technology to produce intellectually stimulating educational toys. There is ample information on this site on the latest brain research. The material is presented in a way that parents can easily understand and the site is simple and easy to navigate. Neurosmith's toys are interactive and focus on fostering specific areas of intelligence like music and language.

The Ounce of Prevention Fund
www.bcm.tmc.edu/civitas/links/ounce.html
The Ounce of Prevention Fund focuses on the importance of early experiences on overall brain development. Their website provides a nice, brief overview of topics associated with early experience and of the brain.

White House Conference on Early Childhood Development and Learning
www.exnet.iastate.edu/Pages/families/nncc/wh/whconf.html
This site provides a wonderful overview of the research findings presented at the 1997 White House review of Early Childhood Development and Learning: "What New Research on the Brain Tells Us About Our Youngest Children." This conference was dedicated to providing a better understanding of the importance of the first few years to child development and learning, and to strengthening efforts that support families and caregivers with young children.

Zero to Three
www.zerotothree.org
Geared for parents of children birth to three years old, this site includes meaningful parent information based on up-to-date research. Topics include understanding developmental assessments and developmental milestones.

Educational

This site provides an overview of educational performance and specific educational advice.

National Association for the Education of Young Children (NAEYC)
www.naeyc.org
National accreditation-granting group for child care institutions in the U.S. Offers a listing of accredited child care centers by zip code or city and state, as well as one-page summaries educating parents and teachers on basic issues such as nutrition and evaluating child care.

Children's Book Recommendations

These sites deal specifically with recommended reading lists for children of different ages.

100 Picture Books Everyone Should Know
www.nypl.org/branch/kids/gloria.html
This site provides the user with the titles and authors of 100 picture books compiled by the New York Public Library. There is no description of the books, but it is a good starting point for parents.

The Children's Literature Web Guide
www.acs.ucalgary.ca/~dkbrown/index.html
This is a wonderful clearinghouse of information on children's literature. This site provides information spanning children's book awards, specific authors and other children's literacy resources on the web. This is one site we recommend as a starting point for any search you might want to begin.

Favorite Books
members.aol.com/ivonavon.booklis.html
This rich site provides parents with lists of award-winning books from past years, as well as a breakdown of books appropriate for different age groups. There are no descriptions of the books, but the titles and authors list should get parents started. Compiled by parent contributors.

Notable Children's Books 1998
www.ala.org/alsc/notable98.html
Posted by the American Library Association, this list provides parents with a board-recommended list of books, a brief description of each book, the name of the illustrator, and the ISBN number. Lists are broken down into age groups (young reader, all ages, older readers).

Music

American Music Conference
www.amc-music.com
This is a national association dedicated to the promotion of the importance of music, music-making and music education. The information on this site has been geared to meet the needs of the general public.

Brooke's Sing a Song Page
http://www.geocities.com/Heartland/Pointe/6261/songmenu.html
One of the only MIDI sites to include the instrumentals as well as the lyrics of favorite children's songs. Classics such as "I'm a Little Teapot" and "Winnie the Pooh" are performed, as well as seasonal songs such as "Frosty the Snowman." Also has links to other electronic music file sites that have a larger selection of children's songs. This site is simple, small and to the point. It's a perfect site to visit with your child.

Fred Koch Children's Music Review
http://www.cowboy.net/~mharper/CMW/Fred/FredKoch.html
This site offers reviews of children's music currently on the market. Although it is narrow in scope, it is also one of the only sites that can help parents wade through the large selection of children's music on the market. Each page is extremely text-intensive, mostly due to the thorough look that Fred Koch takes at each selection. One drawback is that there are no samplings listed along with the reviewed selections. A good site for parents looking to add to their children's music collection.

MENC
www.menc.org/index2.html
The Music Educator's National Conference's mission is to advise "music education as a profession and to ensure that every child in America has access to a balanced, sequential, high-quality education" that includes music as a core subject of study. Although geared to educators, the site does an excellent job of summarizing research on the positive effects of music on young children.

Music Rhapsody
www.musicrhapsody.com
Music Rhapsody, founded by Lynn Kleiner, is an innovative music program for children from infants to eighth grade, based on the Orff Schulwerk philosophy of music — an approach to teaching music based on things children like to do: sing, chant rhymes, dance and play instruments using creativity and imagination. Children experience the joy of making music in a group as they learn the fundamentals of music.

MuSICA
www.musica.uci.edu
MuSICA, the Music and Science Information Computer Archive, is a wonderful resource for parents who want access to the latest in research on music and how music impacts the brain.

Giftedness

Families of the Talented and Gifted
http://www.access.digex.net/~king/tagfam.html
This site provides a community for gifted children and their families, offering different definitions of giftedness by schools, families, doctors, etc. This site aims to educate parents, experts and the general public about giftedness, as well as to provide a forum where issues concerning gifted children can be discussed. A useful links section is included, comprised of websites, organizations and even literature. A must-see for any parent with a gifted child.

Gifted Development Center
www.gifteddevelopment.com
This site is a service of the Institute for the Study of Advanced Development, serving parents, schools and advocacy groups with information about identification, assessment, counseling, learning styles, programs, presentations and resources for gifted children and adults. Also provides links to many other sites. Compiled by an acknowledged leader in this field.

Hoagies' Gifted Education Page
www.ocsc.com/hoagies/gift.html
A comprehensive resource guide for the parenting and education of gifted children. Parents will find information and research about gifted children; links to related websites; recommended books, journals and magazines; online support groups; and stories shared by other parents of gifted children. This is a good introductory site if you believe your child may be gifted.

Assessment and Special Needs

The Autism Society of America
www.autism-society.org
The mission of the Autism Society of America is to promote lifelong access and opportunities for persons within the autism spectrum and their families. Their goal is for this population to be fully included, participating members of their communities through advocacy, public awareness, education and research related to autism.

The Behavior Home Page
www.state.ky.us/agencies/behave/homepage.html
The Kentucky Department of Education and the Department of Special Education and Rehabilitation Counseling and University of Kentucky are collaborating on this web page on student behavior. The purpose is to allow parents, school personnel and other professionals to gain access to information, share effective practices and receive ongoing consultation and technical assistance. Topics include the full range of behavior problems and challenges displayed by children and youth in school and community settings, as well as other behavioral issues that may affect their success in school.

Boys Town Research Registry for Hereditary Hearing Loss
www.boystown.org/deafgene.reg
The Boys Town Research Registry is designed to foster a partnership among families, clinicians and researchers. The site includes a fact sheet index where parents can learn about various issues surrounding deafness, as well as links to personal essays written by parents of deaf children. This is a very good site for parents wanting to learn more about hearing loss.

Developmental Disability Links
www.disdev.stu.umn/index.html
A site committed solely to providing links related to developmental disabilities. Very good selection of links, especially in the legal arena, which is a particular concern for parents attempting to get insurance reimbursement.

The Disability Link Barn
www.accessunlimited.com/developmental_disability.html
A site of the Federal Resource Center for Special Education, Office of Special Education and Rehabilitative Services (OSERS). A great clearinghouse for links.

DREAMMS for Kids, Inc.
www.dreamms.org
A nonprofit clearinghouse for information on assistive technology. This site has numerous articles about adaptive technology devices, the use of assistive technology and how to find funding.

Family Village
www.familyvillage.wisc.edu/index.html
This site contains information on numerous types of disabilities. The site includes information on specific diagnoses, who to contact, where to go to get support (chat with other parents), where to learn more about the diagnosis and other related websites.

The Internet Resources for Special Children (IRSC)
www.accessunlimited.com/
The goal of this organization is to communicate information on the needs of children with disabilities to parents, family members, caregivers, friends, educators and medical professionals.

National Center to Improve Practice in Special Education Through Technology, Media and Materials
www.edc.org/FSC/NCIP
This is a great clearinghouse for articles, products and links related to early childhood education, particularly for those children with special needs. The links to special education sites are wonderful and numerous.

National Information Center for Children and Youth with Disabilities
www.nichcy.org
This government site serves as a clearinghouse for information on disabilities. In addition, publications are posted on the web, which include "political" information, where to go for help, what agencies are available and some of the recent bills and laws. The site would be a good way for parents to get "up to speed" on their child's disability.

Shriners Hospital for Children
www.shrinerspfld.org
A clearinghouse for orthopedic-related information. Great page with numerous links of interest to patients and families. A great place to start for parents of children with orthopedic or prosthetic devices, missing limbs or other health problems and syndromes that the Shriners Hospital addresses.

United Cerebral Palsy
www.ucpa.org/html
A great website for families with children who have cerebral palsy. The resource center is especially helpful, with published literature that is particularly relevant for parents, such as advocacy tips for dealing with school boards or insurance agencies. The information is useful and accurate.

Emergent Literacy

Helping Your Child Learn to Read
http://www.inet.ed.gov/pubs/parents/Reading/index.html
Provided by the U.S. Department of Education, this site focuses literacy skills in children from infancy to 12-years-old. Many reading and writing activities are provided can be completed with supplies from around the house. Numerous tips and suggestions educate parents on how the pre-literate child can learn the basics before even being able to read.

Issues in Literacy Development
www.eduplace.com/rdg/res/literacy/index.html
This site focuses on issues such as emergent literacy and the skills necessary to become a fluent reader. Also discussed are the cognitive aspects of reading (such as phonemics and word identification) as well as strategies for effective teaching. References are given for anyone interested in further research. The material is dry, but extremely informative and well-worth the look through.

Health and Safety

The ABC's of Safe and Healthy Child Care
www.cdc.gov/ncidod/hip/abc/abc.html
Written for caregivers and child care providers, this site includes a published handbook addressing common safety concerns. Parents may reference specific health concerns to get a summary of common symptoms, primary care tips and lists of ways to encourage healthy habits. Also includes links, addresses and phone numbers of regional poison control centers, related federal agencies and other public health/pediatric organizations.

Health Education Resources
www.indiana.edu/%7Eaphs/blthk-12.html
An impressive clearinghouse with a multitude of sites covering a wide range of education, physical fitness, mental health and safety-oriented sites. This is definitely one of the best health-oriented clearinghouses we have seen.

ChildSecure
www.childsecure.com
An impressive health and safety site featuring important information on product warnings and recalls, nutrition news and injury prevention. Current reports and pediatric news stories are listed and can be viewed in their entirety, providing parents with accurate, up-to-date information. An expert panel can be contacted to answer any health questions and a library is kept of past discussion topics. Also available are discussion groups that extend from pregnancy forums to parenting and family discussions.

Kids Health.Org
www.kidshealth.org
Created by medical experts at the Nemours foundation, this site provides information on general health, growth and development, as well as the health care system itself. The 'For Parents' section is useful to any parent with questions about specific medical or health questions. Easy-to-use pull-down menus allow users to select articles on a given subject. Information for each topic is thorough, explaining the mechanism for the illness or injury and typical professional treatment. A helpful 'When to call your pediatrician' section will help you determine when a trip to the doctor may be necessary.

Books and Articles

Brain/Intellectual Development

These books and articles will give you a deeper understanding of the topics discussed in each of our sections. We've included everything from national bestsellers — such as Penelope Leach's "Your Baby & Child," T. Berry Brazelton's "Touchpoints" and Arlene Eisenberg, et. al.'s "What To Expect When You're Expecting" — to reviews of brain development, such as Marian Diamond's "Magic Trees of the Mind" and Terry Deacon's "The Symbolic Species.

Children's Talk
by Garvey, C. (1984). Cambridge, Mass.: Harvard University Press.
Although this book focuses primarily on toddlers and preschoolers, it addresses those elements of talk that have precursors in infancy, namely turn-taking, attention and social signals. Garvey systematically identifies behavioral and psychological dimensions that contribute to verbal exchanges.

Emerging Minds: The Process of Change in Children's Thinking
by Siegler, Robert. (1998). New York: Oxford University Press, Inc.
This book examines how children acquire their thought processes. Siegler theorizes that like the evolution of the species, thoughts are dependent on their success in the environment. This book provides a solid background into current thoughts about how children develop concepts, strategies and skills.

How the Mind Works
by Pinker, S. (1998). New York: W.W. Norton and Company.
Steven Pinker is a foremost researcher and theorist on the development of language. This book has been nominated for numerous awards for good reason: it is an in-depth, easy-to-read approach to describing the latest findings and theories on how we come to speak.

Inside the Brain: Revolutionary Discoveries of How the Mind Works
by Kotulak, R. (1997). Kansas City, Mo.: Andrews McMeel Publishing.
This book is a compilation of articles detailing the changes in brain structure and behaviors. Kotulak interviewed the leaders in neuroscience and brings the information to the reader in a format that is easy to understand.

Magic Trees of the Mind: How to Nurture Your Child's Intelligence, Creativity and Healthy Emotions from Birth Through Adolescence
by Diamond, M., & Hopson, J. (1998). New York: Dutton.
Marian Diamond is an expert in the field of brain development and how the environment affects this development. This book is one of the foremost descriptions of the importance of early experiences on overall development.

The Human Brain: A Guided Tour
edited by Greenfield, S.A. (1997). New York: Basic Books, Inc.
This review provides a detailed look at the structures that comprise the human brain, while also providing a focus on developmental aspects of the brain. Though fascinating, the material can be rather dense.

The Growth of the Mind: And the Endangered Origins of Intelligence
by Greenspan, S.I. (1997). New York: Addison-Wesley.
In this intriguing review of the nature of intelligence, Greenspan focuses on the role of emotional interactions between infant and caregiver and their effects on cognitive abilities. The result is a comprehensive theory of how interpersonal communication styles and family interaction patterns have a long-term effect on the human mind.

The New First Three Years of Life: The Completely Revised and Updated Edition of the Parenting Classic
by White, B.L. (1995). New York, N.Y.: Fireside.
The volume covers areas ranging from the phases of the first three years of life to childrearing topics. Presented in an easy-to-understand manner.

How Babies Talk: The Magic and Mystery of Language in the First Three Years of Life
by Golinkoff, R., and Hirsh-Pasek, K. (1999). New York, N.Y.: Dutton.
This is one of the best books on language development under age three that focuses on the role that parents can play on a child's acquisition of language. Not only does this book give information that you need, but concrete and tangible ideas on activities for language growth. It is divided into three sections: 1) a description of the major milestones that children move through; 2) a 'Try This' section that provides activities for parents to engage in, and 3) a Science Sleuthing section which is a neat link to bridge the gap between science and how that really applies to everyday life.

The Symbolic Species: The Co-evolution of Language and the Brain
by Deacon, T.W. (1997). New York: W.W. Norton and Company.
The author tackles the difficult description of a human's unique capacity for language, providing a detailed description of how the nuances of language acquisition are reflected/controlled by brain development. Although the material is quite detailed, the writing style is relatively light.

Your Child's Growing Mind: A Practical Guide to Brain Development and Learning from Birth to Adolescence
by Healy, J.M. (1994). New York: Doubleday.
As with her other volume, "Endangered Minds," Healy provides a thoughtful review of the literature on brain development, and the risks our children are exposed to, given the environments in which they are raised.

Social-Emotional Development

Baby Steps: The "Whys" of Your Child's Behavior in the First Two Years
by Kopp, C.B. (1994). New York: W.H. Freeman and Company.
Dr. Kopp is a well-respected researcher specializing in the area of social development. Her wonderful book provides the knowledge to understand why your child does some of the things she does in the first two years of life.

Dr. Spock's Baby and Child Care: A Handbook for Parents of Developing Children From Birth Through Adolescence
by Spock, B., & Parker, S.J. (1992). New York: Pocket Books.
This volume is the seminal book on early parenting. Recently revised in collaboration with Dr. Michael Rothenberg, it is a terrific overview and should be included in every parent's library. Dr. Spock presents baby care information in an authoritative, yet reassuring tone. Special attention is given to the role you play as parent, and the role your baby plays in your relationship. Topics covered include prenatal issues, care of your newborn, breast- and bottle-feeding, introduction of solid food and general care throughout the first year. Subsequent sections cover later years of development.

Fatherhood
by Parke, R.D. (1996). Cambridge, Mass.: Harvard University Press.
Parke, a noted researcher on fathers, presents a summary of research related to fatherhood: how fathers change the conceptualization of their role during pregnancy; the effect of pregnancy on marital relationships; how fathers react to their newborns; and the effects of separation or divorce on father-child relationships. In addition, Parke highlights different facets of father-child relationships.

First Feeling: Milestones in the Emotional Life of Your Baby and Child
by Greenspan, S., & Greenspan, N.T. (1985). New York: Penguin Books.
Written for parents, this book discusses the milestones in self-regulation and emotions from birth to four years, offers suggestions for making behavioral observations of infants and offers background and suggestions on the role of support networks in helping parent-infant interactions.

Know Your Child: An Authoritative Guide for Today's Parents
by Chess, S., & Thomas, A. (1997). New York: Basic Books, Inc.
Written exclusively for caregivers, Chess and Thomas use their combined years of research on temperament and social-emotional development to provide practical information about concepts such as temperament, goodness-of-fit and self-esteem. An excellent resource.

Temperament: Individual Differences at the Interface of Biology and Behavior
by Bates, J.E.E., & Wachs, T.D. (1994). Washington, D.C.: APA
This volume is a complete overview of temperament, including the neural bases of temperament, individual differences and the implications of the biological roots of temperament. Although very technical, readers will find a thorough review of recent research findings related to temperament.

The Baby Book: Everything You Need to Know About Your Baby
by Sears, W., & Sears, M. (1993). New York: Little, Brown and Company.
This book starts with how to prepare for birth and goes on to cover everything from breastfeeding to toddler tantrums. The Sears' approach to parenting, called the attachment approach, provides parents with a gentle and reassuring way to deal with the everyday stresses of being a new parent.

The Caring Child
by Eisenberg, N. (1992). Cambridge, Mass.: Harvard University Press.
This book addresses the development of pro-social behavior, including sharing, empathy and sympathy. Although the main focus of the book is on preschoolers, several chapters are particularly relevant for parents of infants.

Raising Your Spirited Child: A Guide for Parents Whose Child Is More Intense, Sensitive, Perceptive, Persistent and Energetic
by Kurcinka, M.S. (1992). New York: Harperperennial Library.
Mary Sheedy Kurcinka, an expert in the parenting field tackles the tough subject of "difficult children." She offers solutions and strategies to successfully cope and more effectively parent on a day-to-day basis.

Touchpoints: The Essential Reference
by Brazelton, T.B. (1992). New York: Addison-Wesley.
This book covers the basic issues that parents must deal with during the first six years, as well as a broad range of special topics, such as allergies, bedwetting, crying, self-esteem, sibling rivalry, speech and hearing problems and toilet training. Main topics are covered in chronological order.

Your Baby and Child: From Birth to Age Five
by Leach, P. (1994). New York: Alfred A. Knopf.
This classic work covers the ins and outs of caring for children up to the age of five. In sections divided by age, Leach touches on topics ranging from feeding, sleeping, teething, illness and crying to comforting, playing, learning, playthings and first-aid.

What to Expect the First Year
by Eisenberg, A., Murkoff, H.E., & Hathaway, S.E. (1989). New York: Workman Publishing.
Written by the same authors who brought you "What to Expect When You're Expecting," this popular, user-friendly volume answers many of the questions of early parenthood. The book is divided into two sections: the first section presents developmental issues in chronological sequence along with a question-and-answer format. It covers such topics as what your baby should be doing at each stage, what you may be concerned about and what is important to know about your baby's health, growth and development. The second half of the book covers special issues, such as illnesses, first-aid, the low-birthweight baby, nutrition, the adopted baby and becoming a father.

Literacy

Phonological Skills and Learning to Read
by Goswami, U., & Bryant, P. (1990). Hove, East Sussex: Lawrence.
The authors of this book are experts in the field of the effects of phonology on reading. This book highlights the relationship between phonological skill and progressions in reading, helping to highlight some of the underpinnings on how children come to learn to read.

The Read Aloud Handbook
by Trelease, J. (1995). New York: Penquin Group.
This is the quintessential guide on the importance of early reading with your child. It is written in an easy-to-read, anecdotal manner and conveys the importance of reading to your child and the effect on later development.

Music

Kids Make Music, Babies Make Music, Too
by Kleiner, L. (1998). Miami, Fla.: Warner Bros. Publications.
This is a wonderful compilation of recommendations on how parents and children can share the joy of music together. Developed by Lynn Kleiner, early childhood pioneer, who is the founder and director of Music Rhapsody, a music program for parents, infants and children.

Learning Sequences in Music: Skill, Content and Patterns
by Gordon, E. (1997). Chicago: GIA Publications.
Although somewhat academic in its approach, Gordon presents a very coherent model for how children come to learn music. Included in his discussion is an examination of the link between early exposure to music and early exposure to language. This volume is excellent for those interested in the theoretical details on how children come to learn and understand music.

Music for Very Little People: 50 Playful Activities for Infants and Toddlers
by Feierabend, J.M., Illustrated by Kramer, G.M. New York: Boosey & Hawkes.
This is a compilation of songs and activities that parents can share with their babies, ranging from songs for bouncing and wiggling to songs for tickling and clapping. The actions are described in detail and the music is provided.

References

Adams, M.J., B.R. Foorman, I. Lundberg, and T. Beeler. *Phonemic Awareness in Young Children: A Classroom Curriculum.* Baltimore: Paul H. Brookes Publishing Co., Inc., 1998.

Althouse, R. *Investigating Mathematics With Young Children.* New York: Teachers College Press, 1994.

Amsterdam, B.K. "Mirror Self-Image Reactions Before Age Two." *Developmental Psychobiology* 5 (1972): 297-305.

Andress, B. *Music for Young Children.* New York: Harcourt Brace and Company, 1998.

Arnold, D.H., C.J. Lonigan, G.J. Whitehurst, and J.N. Epstein. "Accelerating Language Development Through Picture Book Reading: Replication and Extension to a Videotape Training Format." *Journal of Educational Psychology* 86 (1994): 235-243.

Backman, J. "The Role of Psycholinguistic Skills in Reading Acquisition: A Look at Early Readers." *Reading Research Quarterly* 18.4 (1983): 466-479.

Bader, L.A. *Read To Succeed: Literacy Tutor's Manual.* Des Moines: Merrill Prentice Hall, 1998.

Baldwin, D. "Infants' Contribution to the Achievement of Joint Reference." *Child Development* 62 (1991): 875-890.

Baldwin, D.A., and E. Markman. "Establishing Word-Object Relations: A First Step." *Child Development* 60: 381-398.

Baldwin, D.A. "Early Referential Understanding: Infants' Ability to Recognize Referential Acts for What They Are." *Developmental Psychology* 29 (1993): 832-843.

Baldwin, D.A. "Understanding the Link Between Joint Attention and Language." *Joint Attention: Its Origins and Role in Development.* Ed. Chris Moore and Philip J.Dunham. Hillsdale, NJ: Lawrence Erlbaum Associates, Inc., 1995. 131-158.

Bamford, R.A, and J.V. Kristo. *Making Facts Come Alive: Choosing Quality Nonfiction Literature.* Norwood, MA: Christopher-Gordon Publishers, Inc., 1998. 372.

Barclay, K. "Literacy Begins at Birth: What Caregivers Can Learn from Parents of Children Who Read Early." *Young Children* 50.4 (1995): 24-28.

Barrett, M., Harris, and L. Chasin. "Early Lexical Development and Maternal Speech: A Comparison of Children's Initial and Subsequent Use of Early Words." *Journal of Child Language* 18 (1991): 21-40.

Bates, E. "Language About Me and You: Pronominal Reference of the Emergent Concept of Self." *The Self in Transition: Infancy to Childhood.* Ed. D. Cicchetti and M. Beeghly. The John D. and Catherine T. MacArthur Foundation Series on Mental Health and Development. Chicago: University of Chicago Press, 1990. 165-182.

Bates, E., D. Thal, and J.S. Janowsky. "Early Language Development and Its Neural Correlates." *Handbook of Neuropsychology.* Ed. I. Rapin and S. Segalowitz. Vol. 7. Amsterdam: Elsevie, 1992. 69-110.

Bates, E., D. Thal, D.Trauner, J. Fenson, D. Aram, J. Eisele, and R. Nass. "From First Words to Grammar In Children With Focal Brain Injury." *Developmental Neuropsychology* 13.3 (1997): 275-343.

Bates, E., I. Bretherton, L. Snyder, M. Beeghly, C. Shore, S. McNew, V. Carlson, C. Williamson, and A. Garrison. *From First Words to Grammar: Individual Differences and Dissociable Mechanisms.* New York: Cambridge University Press, 1988.

Bates, E., V. Marchman, D. Thal, L. Fenson, P. Dale, S. Reznik, J. Reilly, and J. Hartung. "Developmental and Stylistic Variation in the Composition of Early Vocabulary." *Journal of Child Language* 21 (1994): 85-123.

Bauer, P.J. "Development of Memory in Early Childhood." *The Development of Memory in Childhood: Studies in Developmental Psychology.* Ed. Nelson Cowan, et al. Hove, England UK: Psychology Press/Erlbaum (UK) Taylor and Francis, 1997. 83-111.

Bauer, P.J., and J.M Mandler. "Putting the Horse Before the Cart: The Use of Temporal Order in Recall of Events By One-Year-Old Children." *Developmental Psychology* 28 (1992): 441-452.

Bauer, P.J., and J.M. Mandler. "One Thing Follows Another: Effects of Temporal Structure on 1- to 2-year-olds' Recall of Events." *Developmental Psychology* 25 (1989): 197-206.

Bauer, P.J., and S. Wewerka. "One- to Two-Year-Olds' Recall of Events: The More Expressed, the More Impressed." *Journal of Experimental Child Psychology* 59 (1995): 475-477.

Bauer, Patricia J. "What Do Infants Recall of Their Lives? Memory for Specific Events By One- to Two-Year-Olds." *American Psychologist* 51 (1996): 29-41.

Bergman, A., and I. S. Lefcourt. "Self-Other Action Play: A Window into the Representational World of the Infant." *Children*

At Play. Ed. A. Slade and D. P. Wolf. New York: Oxford University Press, 1994. 133-147.

Black, J.E., A.M. Sirevaag, and W.T. Greenough. "Complex Experience Promotes Capillary Formation in Young Rat Visual Cortex." *Neuroscience Letters* 83 (1987): 351-355.

Black, J.E., A.M. Zelazny, and W.T. Greenough. "Capillary and Mitochondrial Support of Neural Plasticity in Adult Rat Visual Cortex." *Experimental Neurology* 111 (1991): 204-209.

Black, J.E., M. Polinsky, and W.T. Greenough. "Progressive Failure of Cerebral Angiogenesis Supporting Neural Plasticity in Aging Rats." *Neurobiology of Aging* 10 (1989): 353-358.

Blatchford, P. "Associations Between Pre-School Reading Related Skills and Later Reading Achievement." *British Educational Research Journal* 13.1 (1987): 15-23.

Block, C. "Strategy Instruction in a Literature-Based Reading Program." *The Elementary School Journal* 94 (1993): 140-150.

Bloom, L. *The Transition from Infancy to Language: Acquiring the Power of Expression.* New York: Cambridge University Press, 1993.

Bransford, J., R. Sherwood, N. Vye, and J. Rieser. "Teaching Thinking and Problem Solving." *American Psychologist* 41 (1986): 1078-1089.

Brazelton, T.B. *Touchpoints: The Essential Reference.* New York: Addison-Wesley, 1992.

Bremner, J.G. *Infancy* 2nd ed. Cambridge: Blackwell Publishers, Inc., 1994.

Brightbill, M. *The Long-Term Effects of Remedial Reading Instruction.* New Brunswick: Graduate School of Education, 1971.

Bromley, K.D. *Language Arts: Exploring Connections.* 3rd ed. Des Moines: Allyn and Bacon, 1998.

Brooks-Gunn, Jeanne, and Michael Lewis. "The Development of Early Visual Self Recognition in Infancy." *Developmental Review* 4 (1984): 215-239.

Brown, A.L. "Metacognitive Development and Reading." *Theoretical Issues in Reading Comprehension.* Hillsdale, N.J.: Lawrence Erlbaum, 1980.

Brown, A.L., J.L. Campione, and J.D. Day. "Learning to Learn: On Training Students to Learn from Texts." *Educational Researcher* 10 (1981): 14-21.

Bryant, P.E., M. MacLean, L.L. Bradley, and J. Crossland. "Rhyme and Alliteration, Phoneme Detection, and Learning to Read." *Developmental Psychology* 26 (1990): 429-438.

Bullock, M., and P. Lutkenhaus. "The Development of Volitional Behavior in the Toddler Years." *Child Development* 59 (1989): 664-674.

Bus, A.G., M.H. Ijzendoorn, and A. Pelligrini. "Joint Book Reading Makes for Success in Learning to Read: A Meta-Analysis on Intergenerational Transmission of Literacy." *Review of Educational Research* 65 (1995): 1-21.

Bushnell, M. *I/T/A/ News.* New York: Initial Teaching Alphabet Publications, Inc., 1971.

Byrne, B., and R. Fielding-Barnsley. "Evaluation of a Program to Teach Phonemic Awareness to Young Children: A 2- and 3-Year Follow-Up and a New Preschool Trial." *Journal of Educational Psychology* 87 (1995): 488-503.

Caldwell, S.T. "Highly Gifted Preschool Readers." *Journal for the Education of the Gifted* 8 (1985): 165-174.

Carpenter, M., N. Akhtar, and M. Tomasello. "Fourteen- Through 18-Month-Old Infants Differentially Imitate Intentional and Accidental Actions." *Infant Behavior and Development.* (1998): 315-330.

Ceprano, M.A. *The Effects of Two Sight Word Teaching Methods on Featural Attention of Children Beginning to Read.* Paper presented at the Annual Meeting of the American Educational Research Association. Washington, D.C.: 1987.

Chapman, K., L.B. Leonard, and C.B. Mervis. "The Effects of Feedback on Young Children's Inappropriate Word Usage." *Journal of Child Language* 13 (1986): 101-111.

Chen, J., E.M. Isberg, and M. Krechevsky. *Project Spectrum: Early Learning Activities.* New York: Teachers College Press, 1998.

Chugani, H.T. "A Critical Period of Brain Development: Studies of Cerebral Glucose Utilization with PET." *Preventive Medicine* 27 (1998): 184-188.

Cohen, L.B. "An Information-Processing Approach to Infant Perception and Cognition." *The Development of Sensory, Motor and Cognitive Capacities in Early Infancy: From Perception to Cognition.* Ed. Simion, Francesca and George Butterworth. Hove, England UK: Psychology Press/Erlbaum (UK) Taylor and Francis, 1998: 277-300.

Cohen, L.B., L.J. Rundell, B.A. Spellman, and C.H. Cashon. "Infants' Perception of Causal Chains." *Psychological Science* (1999, in press).

Cohen, L.B., and L.M. Oakes. "How Infants Perceive a Simple Causal Event." *Developmental Psychology* 29 (1993): 421-433.

Cole, M., and S.R. Cole. *The Development of Children*. 3rd ed. New York: W. H. Freeman and Company, 1996.

Cornell, E.H., M. Senechal, and L.S. Broda. "Recall of Picture Books By 3-Year-Old Children: Testing and Repetition Effects in Joint Reading Activities." *Journal of Educational Psychology* 77 (1988): 349-361.

Cryer, D., T. Harms, and B. Bourland. *Active Learning for Infants*. New York: Addison-Wesley Publishing Company, 1987.

Cryer, D., T. Harms, and B. Bourland. *Active Learning for Ones*. New York: Addison-Wesley Publishing Company, 1987.

Curtis, S.R. *The Joy of Movement in Early Childhood*. New York: Teachers College Press, 1982.

Darnell, C.D., and W.L. Goodwin. *The Kindergarten Child 1971 or the Class of 1984*. Paper presented at the 83rd Annual Meeting of the American Psychological Association, Chicago, Illinois. Chicago: American Psychological Association, 1975.

Dawson, G., and K.W. Fischer. *Human Behavior and the Developing Brain*. New York: The Guilford Press, 1994.

Dawson, G., H. Panagiotides, L.G. Klinger and D. Hill. "The Role of Frontal Lobe Functioning in the Development of Infant Self-Regulatory Behavior." *Brain and Cognition* 20 (1992): 152-175.

de Boysson-Bardies, B. and M.M. Vihman. "Adaptation to Language: Evidence from Babbling and First Words in Four Languages." *Language* 67 (1991): 297-319.

De Temple, J.M., and P.O. Tabors. *Children's Story Retelling as a Predictor of Early Reading Achievement*. Paper presented at the Biennial Meeting of the International Society for the Study of Behavioral Development. Quebec City, Quebec, Canada: International Society for the Study of Behavioral Development, 1996.

Deliège, I., and J. Sloboda. *Musical Beginnings: Origins and Development of Musical Competence*. New York: Oxford University Press, 1996.

DeLoache, J.S., D.H. Uttal, and S.L. Pierroutsakos. "The Development of Early Symbolization: Educational Implications." *Learning and Instruction* 8 (1998): 325-339.

DeLoache, J.S., S.L. Pierroutsakos, D.H. Uttal, K.S. Rosengren, and A. Gottlieb. "Grasping the Nature of Pictures." *Psychological Science* 9 (1998): 205-210.

DeLoache, J.S., and O.A. Mendoza. "Joint Picturebook Interactions of Mothers of 1-Year-Old Children." *British Journal of Developmental Psychology* 5 (1987): 111-123.

Department of Education. Council for Educational Development and Research. *What We Know About Reading Teaching and Learning: EdTalk*. Washington, D.C.: Council for Educational Development and Research, 1997.

Diamond, A. "Neuropsychological Insights into the Meaning of Object Concept Development." *The Epigenesis of Mind: Essays on Biology and Cognition. The Jean Piaget Symposium series*. Ed. Susan Carey and Rochel Gelman, et al. Hillsdale, NJ: Lawrence Erlbaum Associates, Inc., 1991: 67-110.

Diamond, M., and J. Hopson. *Magic Trees of the Mind: How to Nurture Your Child's Intelligence, Creativity, and Healthy Emotions from Birth Through Adolescence*. New York: Penguin Books, 1998.

Dixon, W., and C. Shore. "Temperamental Predictors of Linguistic Style During Multiword Acquisition." *Infant Behavior and Development* 20 (1997): 99-103.

Dunn, J., and C. Wooding. "Play in the Home and its Implications for Learning." *The Biology of Play*. Ed. B. Tizard and D. Harvey. London: Spastics International Medical Publications/Heinemann Medical Books, 1977.

Dunn, J., and N. Dale. "I a Daddy: 2-year-olds' Collaboration in Joint Pretend with Sibling and with Mother." *Symbolic Play: The Development of Social Understanding*. Ed. I. Bretherton. Orlando: Academic Press, 1984. 131-158.

Durkin, D. *Early Reading Instruction—Is It Advantageous?* Paper Presented at the Annual Symposium of the Jean Piaget Society. Philadelphia: Jean Piaget Society, 1987.

Edelen-Smith, P. "How Now Brown Cow: Phoneme Awareness Activities for Collaborative Classrooms." *Intervention in School and Clinic* 33.2 (1997): 103-111.

Eisenberg, N., and R.A. Fabes. "Prosocial Development." *Handbook of Child Psychology*. 5th edition. Vol. 3. New York: Wiley and Sons, 1998. 701-778.

Eldredge, L. "An Experiment with a Modified Whole Language Approach in First Grade Classrooms." *Reading Research and Instruction* 30.3 (1991): 21-28.

Elley, W.B. "Vocabulary Acquisition From Listening to Stories." *Reading Research Quarterly* 24 (1989): 175-187.

Elman, J.L., E.A. Bates, M.H. Johnson, A. Karmiloff-Smith, D. Parisi, and K. Plunkett. *Rethinking Innateness*. Cambridge: MIT Press, 1997.

Emde, R.N. "Development Terminable and Interminable: Innate and Motivational Factors from Infancy." *International Journal of Psychoanalysis* 69 (1988): 23-25.

Ericson, B., M. Hubler, T. Bean, C. Smith, and J. Mckenzie. "Increasing Critical Reading in Junior High Classrooms." *Journal of Reading* 30 (1987): 430-439.

Feierabend, J.M. *First Steps in Music for Nursery and Preschool*. Simsbury, CT: First Steps in Music, Inc., 1995.

Feierabend, J.M., and G.M. Kramer. *Music for Very Little People: 50 Playful Activities for Infants and Toddlers*. Farmingdale, NY: Boosey & Hawkes, Inc., 1986.

Feldman, S.C. *Analyzing Reading Growth of Disadvantaged Children Through Longitudinal Study of Several Reading Measures*. Paper presented at the meeting of the American Educational Research Association. New York: American Educational Research Association, 1971.

Fenson, L., and D.S. Ramsay. "Decentration and Integration in the Child's Play in the Second Year." *Child Development* 51 (1980): 171-178.

Fernald, A., and P.K. Kuhl. "Acoustic Determinants of Infant Preference for Motherese Speech." *Infant Behavior and Development* 10 (1987): 279-293.

Flavell, J.H. "Cognitive Monitoring." *Children's Oral Communication Skills*. New York: Academic Press, 1981.

Fletcher, P., and B. MacWhinney. *The Handbook of Child Language*. Cambridge: Blackwell Publishers, Inc., 1996.

Flood, J., and D. Lapp. "Reporting Reading Progress: A Comparison Portfolio for Parents." *Reading Teacher* 42.7 (1989): 508-514.

Foley, C.L. *Four Longitudinal Studies of the Starter Approach, a Beginning Reading Strategy for Nonreaders*. Paper presented at the 32nd Annual Meeting of the International Reading Association. Anaheim, CA: International Reading Association, 1987.

Fountas, I.C, and G.S. Pinnell. *Guided Reading: Good First Teaching for All Children*. Portsmouth, N.H.: Heinemann, 1996.

Fox, N.A., and M.A. Bell. "Electrophysiological Indices of Frontal Lobe Development." *Annals of the New York Academy of Sciences* 608 (1990): 677-698.

Fox, N.A., and R.J. Davidson. "Hemispheric Substrates of Affect: A Developmental Model." *The Psychobiology of Affective Development*. Ed. N.A. Fox and R.J. Davidson. Hillsdale, NJ: Lawrence Erlbaum, 1984. 353-381.

Freppon, P., and K. Dahl. "Learning About Phonics in a Whole Language Classroom." *Language Arts* (March 1991): 190-197.

Freppon, P.A, and E. McIntyre. *From Emergent to Conventional Reading: Similarities and Differences in Children's Learning in Skills-Based and Whole Language Classrooms*. Paper Presented at the Annual Meeting of the American Educational Research Association. Washington, D.C.: Department of Education, American Educational Research Association, 1997.

Gallup, G.G. "Chimpanzees: Self-recognition." *Science* 157 (1970): 86f.

Gallup, G.G. "Self-recognition in Primates." *American Psychologist* 32 (1977): 329-338.

Garvey, C. Play. Cambridge: Harvard University Press, 1977.

Gentry, J. Richard. *Sped ... is a Four-Letter Word*. Portsmouth, NH: Heinemann, 1987.

Gibson, K.G. "Myelination and Behavioral Development: A Comparative Perspective on Questions of Neoteny, Altriciality, and Intelligence." *Brain Maturation and Cognitive Development*. Ed. K. Gibson and A. Petersen. New York: Aldine De Gruyter, 1991.

Gipe, J.P. *Multiple Paths to Literacy: Corrective Reading Techniques for Classroom Teachers*. 4th Ed. Old Tappan, NJ: Prentice Hall, 1998.

Goldfield, B. "The Contributions of Child and Caregiver to Referential and Expressive Language." *Applied Psycholinguistics* 8 (1987): 267-280.

Goldfield, B., and J.S. Reznik. "Early Lexical Acquisition: Rate, Content, and the Vocabulary Spurt." *Journal of Child Language* 17 (1990): 171-183.

Goldstein, J.H. *Toys, Play, and Child Development*. Cambridge: University of Cambridge Press, 1995.

Goodman, K. "Reading: A Psycholinguistic Guessing Game." *Theoretical Models and Processor of Reading*. Newark, DE: International Reading Association, 1976. 497-508.

Goodman, K. *Phonics Phacts.* Portsmouth, NH: Heinemann, 1993.

Goodman, K. *What's Whole In Whole Language?* Portsmouth, NH: Heinemann, 1986.

Goodwyn, S.W., and L.P. Acredolo. "Symbolic Gesture Versus Word: Is There a Modality Advantage for Onset of Symbol Use?" *Child Development* 64 (1993): 688-701.

Graziano, A.B., M. Peterson, and G.L. Shaw. "Enhanced Learning of Proportional Math Through Music Training and Spatial-Temporal Training." *Neurological Research* 21 (1999): 139-152.

Greenberg, M.T., and J.L. Snell. "Brain Development and Emotional Development: The Role of Teaching in Organizing the Frontal Lobe." *Emotional Development and Emotional Intelligence.* Ed. P. Salovey and D.J. Sluyter. New York: Basic Books, 1997.

Greenspan, S.I. *The Growth of the Mind: And the Endangered Origins of Intelligence.* New York: Addison-Wesley Publishing Company, Inc., 1996.

Greenspan, S.I., and A.F. Lieberman. "Representational Elaboration and Differentiation: A Clinical-Quantitative Approach to the Clinical Assessment of 2- to 4-Year-Olds." *Children at Play.* Ed. A. Slade and D.P. Wolf. New York: Oxford University Press, 1994. 3-32.

Griffith, P.L., and J.P. Klesius. "The Effect of Phonemic Awareness on the Literacy Development of First Grade Children in a Traditional or a Whole Language Classroom." *Journal of Research In Childhood Education* 6.2 (1992): 85-92.

Gromko, J.E., and A.S. Poorman. "Effects of Music Training on Preschoolers' Spatial-Temporal Task Performance." *Journal of Research in Music Education* 46.2 (Summer, 1998): 173-181.

Hampson, J., and K. Nelson. "The Relation of Maternal Language to Variation in Rate and Style of Language Acquisition." *Journal of Child Language* 20 (1993): 313-342.

Hanna, E., and A.N. Meltzoff. "Peer Imitation By Toddlers in Laboratory, Home, and Day-Care Contexts: Implications for Social Learning and Memory." *Developmental Psychology* 29 (1993): 701-710.

Hanson, R.A, and D. Farrell. "The Long-Term Effects on High School Seniors of Learning to Read in Kindergarten." *Reading Research Quarterly* 30.4 (1995): 908-933.

Hanson, R.A, E. Siegel, and D. Farrell. *The Long-Term Effects of Learning to Read in Kindergarten: A Twelve Year Follow-Up Study.* Paper Presented at U.S. Department of Education. Washington, D.C.: U.S. Department of Education, 1988.

Harris, A., and E. Sipay. *How to Increase Reading Ability: A Guide to Developmental and Remedial Methods.* White Plains, NY: Longman, 1985.

Harris, M., M. Barrett, D. Jones, and S. Brookes. "Linguistic Input and Early Word Meaning." *Journal of Child Language* 15 (1988): 77-94.

Hart, B., and T.R. Risely. *Meaningful Differences in the Everyday Experience of Young American Children.* Baltimore: Paul H. Brookes Publishing Co., Inc., 1995.

Harter, S. "The Development of Self-Representations." *Handbook of Child Psychology* 5th Ed. Vol. 3. New York: Wiley and Sons, 1998. 553-618.

Haussler, M.M., and Y.M. Goodman. "Resources for Involving Parents in Literacy Development." *Clearinghouse on Reading and Communication Skills.* 1984. 11.

Herschkowitz, N., J. Kagan, and K. Zilles. "Neurobiological Bases of Behavioral Development in the First Year." *Neuropediatrics* 28 (1997): 296-306.

Heyge, L., and A. Sillick. "Music: A Natural Way to Play with Babies." *Early Childhood Connections* (Fall 1998): 8-13.

Hirsh-Pasek, K., and R.M. Golinkoff. *The Origins of Grammar: Evidence from Early Language Comprehension.* Cambridge: MIT Press, 1999.

Hirst, W.E. *Prediction of Reading Success.* Paper Presented at the Conference of the American Educational Research Association. Minneapolis: American Educational Research Association, 1970.

Homgren, K., B. Lindblom, G. Aurelius, B. Jalling, and R. Zetterström. "Precursors of Early Speech: On the Phonetics of Infant Vocalization." *Wenner-Gren International Symposium Series* Vol. 44. Ed. B., Lindblom and R. Zetterström. New York: Stockton Press, 1986. 51-63.

Huttenlocher J., W. Haight, A. Bryk, M. Seltzer, and T. Lyons. "Early Vocabulary Growth: Relation to Language Input and Gender." *Developmental Psychology* 27 (1991): 236-248.

Huttenlocher, P.R. "Synaptic Density in Human Frontal Cortex – Developmental Changes and Effects of Aging." *Brain Research* 163 (1979): 195-205.

Huttenlocher, P.R., C. de Courten, LJ Garey, and H. Van Der Loos. "Synaptogenesis in Human Visual Cortex – Evidence for Synapse Elimination During Normal Development." *Neuroscience Letters* 33 (1982). 247-252.

Johnson, M.H. *Developmental Cognitive Neuroscience.* Cambridge: Blackwell Publishers, 1997.

Johnson, M.H. *Brain Development and Cognition.* Cambridge: Blackwell Publishers, 1996.

Juel, C. "The Rule of Decoding in Early Literacy Instruction and Assessment." *Assessment for Instruction in Early Literacy.* Englewood Cliffs: NJ Prentice Hall: Morrow and Smith, 1990.

Kagan, J. *The Second Year: The Emergence of Self-Awareness.* Cambridge: Harvard University Press, 1981.

Karnofsky, F., and T. Weiss. *How To Prepare Your Child for Kindergarten.* Paper Presented at the Sixteenth Annual Meeting of the International Reading Association. Atlantic City: International Reading Association, 1971.

Karweit, N. "The Effects of a Story Reading Program on the Vocabulary and Story Comprehension Skills of Disadvantaged Pre-kindergarten and Kindergarten Students." *Center for Research on Elementary and Middle Schools.* 1989. 1-21.

Kemler-Nelson, D.G., K. Hirsh-Pasek, P. Jusczyk, and K. Wright Cassidy. "How Prosodic Cues in Motherese Might Assist Language Learning." *Journal of Child Language* 16 (1989): 55-68.

Koopmans-van Beinunm, F.J., and J.M. van der Stelt. "Precursors of Early Speech: Early Stages in the Development of Speech Movements." *Wenner-Gren International Symposium Series.* Vol. 44. Ed. B., Lindblom and R. Zetterström. New York: Stockton Press. 37-50.

Kopp, C.B. *Baby Steps: The "Whys" of Your Child's Behavior in the First Two Years.* New York: W.H. Freeman and Company, 1994.

Kopp, C.B. "Regulation of Distress and Negative Emotions: A Developmental View." *Developmental Psychology* 25 (1989): 343-354.

Krasnegor, N.A., G.R. Lyon, and P.S. Goldman-Rakic. *Development of the Prefrontal Cortex: Evolution, Neurobiology, and Behavior.* Baltimore: Paul H. Brookes Publishing Co., Inc., 1997.

Krumhansl, C.L., and P.W.C. Jusczyk. "Infant's Perception of Phrase Structure in Music." *Psychological Science* 1 (1990): 70-73.

Kurcinka, M.S. *Raising Your Spirited Child: A Guide for Parents Whose Child Is More Intense, Sensitive, Perceptive, Persistent, and Energetic.* New York: Harperperennial Library, 1992.

Lansky, V. *Games Babies Play From Birth to Twelve Months.* Deephaven, MN: The Book Peddlers, 1993.

Larsen, J.J. *Yes, Head Start Improves Reading!* Unpublished research report done at University of Florida, Gainesville, 1972.

Leach, P. *Your Baby & Child: From Birth to Age Five.* New York: Alfred A. Knopf, Inc., 1994.

Lesgoid, A.M., and L.B. Resnick. "How Reading Disabilities Develop: Perspectives from a Longitudinal Study." *Theory and Research in Learning Disability.* New York: Plenum, 1982. 155-187.

Leslie, L. "Developmental-Interactive Approach to Reading Assessment." *Reading and Writing Quarterly* 9.1 (1993): 5-30.

Lewis, M. "Self-Conscious Emotions: Embarrassment, Pride, Shame, and Guilt." *Handbook of Emotions.* Ed. M. Lewis and J.M. Haviland. New York: Guilford Press, 1993.

Lewis, M., and J. Brooks-Gunn. *Social Cognition and the Acquisition of Self.* New York: Plenum Press, 1979.

Liberman. I., and A. Liberman. "Whole Language Versus Code Emphasis." *Annals of Dyslexia* 40 (1990): 51-76.

Lie, A. "Effects of a Training Program for Stimulating Skills in Word Analysis in First-Grade Children." *Reading Research Quarterly* 26.3 (1991): 234-250.

Lieberman, A.F. *The Emotional Life of the Toddler.* New York: The Free Press, 1993.

Lundberg. "Learning to Read." *School Research Newsletter.* Vol. 1. (1984). Sweden: National Board of Education in Sweden, 1984.

Lyytinen, P., A.M. Poikkeus, and M.L. Laakso. "Language and Symbolic Play in Toddlers." *International Journal of Behavioral Development* 21 (1997): 289-302.

MacGillivray, L. "'I've Seen You Read': Reading Strategies in a First-Grade Class." *Journal of Research in Childhood Education* 11.2 (1997): 135-146.

Maclean, M. "Rhymes, Nursery Rhymes, and Reading in Early Childhood." *Merrill-Palmer Quarterly* v33 (1987): 255-81.

Madole, K.L., and L.B. Cohen. "The Role of Object Parts in Infants' Attention to Form-Function Correlations." *Developmental Psychology* 31 (1995): 637-648.

Madole, K.L., L.M. Oakes, and L.B. Cohen. "Developmental Changes in Infants' Attention to Function and Form-Function Correlations." *Cognitive Development* 8 (1993): 189-209.

Mahler, M.S. "On Human Symbiosis and the Vicissitudes of Individuation." *Journal of the American Psychoanalytic Association* 15 (1967): 740-763.

Mandler, J.M. "Development of Categorization: Perceptual and Conceptual Categories." *Infant Development: Recent Advances*. Ed. Gavin Bremner, Alan Slater, et al. Hove, England UK: Psychology Press/Erlbaum (Uk) Taylor and Francis, 1997. 163-189.

Mandler, J.M. "How to Build a Baby: II. Conceptual Primitives." *Psychological Review* 99 (1992): 587-604.

Mandler, J.M., and L. McDonough. "Studies in Inductive Inference in Infancy." *Cognitive Psychology* 37 (1998): 60-96.

Marchman, V., and E. Bates. "Continuity in Lexical and Morphological Development: A Test of the Critical Mass Hypothesis." *Journal of Child Language* 21 (1994): 339-366.

Martin, E. *Baby Games: The Joyful Guide to Child's Play from Birth to Three Years*. Philadelphia: Running Press, 1988.

Mautte, L.A. "The Effects of Adult-Interactive Behaviors Within the Context of Repeated Storybook Readings Upon the Language Development and Selected Prereading Skills of Pre-kindergarten At Risk Students." *Florida Educational Research Council Research Bulletin* 22.3 (1990).

McCabe, T.A. *The Distar Reading and Language Program: A Study of Its Effectiveness as a Method for the Initial Teaching of Reading*. Diss. University of Massachusetts, 1974.

McCall, R.B. "Exploratory Manipulation and Play in the Human Infant." *Monographs of the Society for Research in Child Development* Series 155 Vol. 39. Chicago: The University of Chicago Press, 1974.

McCune, L., D. DiPane, R. Fireoved, and M. Fleck. "Play: A Context for Mutual Regulation Within Mother-Child Interaction." *Children at Play*. Ed. A. Slade and D.P. Wolf. New York: Oxford University Press, 1994. 148-168.

McCune-Nicholich, L. "Toward Symbolic Functioning: Structure of Early Pretend Games and Potential Parallels with Language." *Child Development* 52 (1981): 785-797.

McGuiness, D., C. McGuinness, and J. Donohue. "Phonological Training and the Alphabet Principle: Evidence for Reciprocal Causality." *Reading Research Quarterly* 30 (1995): 830-852.

McLean, P.D. *The Triune Brain in Evolution: Role in Paleocerebral Functions*. Plenum Press: New York, 1990.

Mehler, J., P. Jusczyk, G. Lambertz, N. Halsted, J. Bertoncini, and C. Amiel Tison. "A Precursor of Language Acquisition in Young Infants." *Cognition* 29 (1988): 143-178.

Meltzoff, A.N. "Infant Imitation and Memory: Nine-Month-Olds in Immediate and Deferred Tests." *Child Development* 59 (1988): 1221-1229.

Meltzoff, A.N. "Understanding the Intentions of Others: Re-Enactment of Intended Acts By 18-Month-Old Children." *Developmental Psychology* 31 (1995): 838-850.

Meltzoff, A.N. "What Infant Memory Tells Us About Infantile Amnesia: Long-Term Recall and Deferred Imitation." *Journal of Experimental Child Psychology* 59 (1995): 497-515.

Meyer, L.A. *Direct Instruction: A Project Follow Through Success Story. Technical Report No. 302*. Illinois University, Urbana. Center for the Study of Reading. Cambridge: Bolt, Beranek and Newman, Inc., 1983.

Mills, D.M., S.A. Coffey-Corina, and H.J. Neville. "Maturational and Competence-Related Factors in the Development of Cerebral Specializations for Language." *Journal of Cognitive Neuroscience* 5 (1992): 326-342.

Mills, D.M., S.A. Coffey-Corina, and H.J. Neville. "Language Abilities and Cerebral Specializations in 10-20 Month Olds." *Neurocorrelates of Early Cognition and Linguistic Development*. Chair C. Nelson. Symposium Presented at the Biennial Meeting of the Society for Research in Child Development. Seattle: Society for Research and Development, 1991.

Mills, H., T. O'Keefe, D. Stephens. *Looking Closely. Exploring the Role of Phonics in a Whole Language Class*. Urbana, IL: National Council of Teachers of English, 1987.

Molfese, D.L. "Electrophysiological Correlates of Word Meanings in 14-Month-Old Human Infants." *Developmental Neuropsychology* 5 (1989): 79-103.

Moog, H. *The Musical Experience of the Pre-School Child*. London: Schott and Company, Ltd., 1976.

Morris, S.M. *The Long-Term Effects of Remediation in Reading Over a Four-Year Period*. M.A. Thesis, Kean College of New Jersey, 1983.

Moser, S.E. *Early Reading. Parents Who Want To, Can and Should Help Their Children Acquire Early Reading at Home*. Paper presented at the Annual Meeting of the American Educational Research Association. Chicago: American Research Association, 1997.

Moustatfa, M. "Children's Productive Phonological Re-coding." *Reading Research Quarterly* 30.3 (1995): 464-476.

Munger, E.M, and S.J. Bowdon. *Beyond Peek-a-Boo and Pat-a-Cake: Activities for Baby's First 24 Months*. Clinton, NJ: New Win Publishing, Inc., 1993.

Murray, B.A. *Developing Phonological Awareness through Alphabet Books*. Paper Presented at the Annual Meeting of the National Reading Conference. National Reading Conference, 1993.

Namy, L.L., and S.R. Waxman. "Words and Gestures: Infants' Interpretations of Different Forms of Symbolic Reference." *Child Development* 69 (1998): 295-308.

Neisser, U. "Two Perceptually Given Aspects of the Self and Their Development." Spec. Issue: The Development of Self: The First Three Years. *Developmental Review* 11 (1991): 197-209.

Nelson, K. *Narratives from the Crib*. Cambridge: Harvard University Press, 1989.

Nelson, K. "Structure and Strategy in Learning to Talk." *Monographs of the Society for Research in Child Development* ser. 149. 38.1-2 (1973).

Newman, J.M. *Whole Language-Theory in Use*. Portsmouth, NH: Heinemann, 1985.

Nicholich, L. "Beyond Sensorimotor Intelligence: Assessment of Symbolic Maturity Through Analysis of Pretend Play." *Merrill-Palmer Quarterly* 23 (1977): 89-102.

Notari-Syverson, A., R.E. O'Connor, and P.F. Vadasy. *Ladders to Literacy: A Preschool Activity Book*. Baltimore, MD: Paul H. Brookes Publishing Co., Inc., 1998.

Oakes, L.M., and L.B. Cohen. "Infant Perception of a Causal Event." *Cognitive Development* 5 (1990): 193-207.

Oakes, L.M., J. M. Plumert, J.M. Lansink, and J.D. Merryman. "Evidence for Task-Dependent Categorization in Infancy." *Infant Behavior and Development* 19 (1996): 425-440.

Odean, K. *Great Books for Girls*. New York: Ballantine Books, 1997.

Oller, D.K. "The Emergence of the Sounds of Speech in Infancy." *Child Phonology: Production* Vol. 1. Eds. G.H. Yeni-Komshian, J.F. Kavanagh, and C.A. Ferguson. New York: Academic Press, 1980. 93-112.

Papou_ek, M. "Determinants of Responsiveness to Infant Vocal Expression of Emotional State." *Infant Behavior and Development* 12 (1989): 505-522.

Papou_ek, M., and H. Papou_ek. "Preverbal Vocal Communication from Zero to One: Preparing the Ground for Language Acquisition." *Perspectives on Infant Development: Contributions from German-Speaking Countries*. Ed. M. E. Lamb and H. Keller. Hillsdale, New Jersey: Erlbaum, 1991. 299-328.

Papou_ek, M., H. Papou_ek, and M.H. Bornstein. "The Naturalistic Vocal Environment of Young Infants: On the Significance of Homogeneity and Variability in Parental Speech." *Social Perception in Infants*. Ed. T. Field and N. Fox. Norwood, New Jersey: Ablex, 1985. 269-297.

Payne, A. C., G.J. Whitehurst, and A. Angell. "The Role of Home Literacy Environment in the Development of Language Ability in Preschool Children from Low-Income Families." *Early Childhood Research Quarterly* 9 (1994): 427-440.

Pearson, B. and S. Fernandez. "Patterns of Interaction in the Lexical Growth in Two Languages." *Language Learning* 44 (1994): 617-653.

Pearson, B., S. Fernandez, V. Lewedeg, and K. Oller. "The Relation of Input Factors to Lexical Learning by Bilingual Infants." *Applied Psycholinguistics* 18 (1997): 1-58.

Phillips, Linda M. "Longitudinal Effects of Early Literacy Concepts on Reading Achievement: A Kindergarten Intervention and Five-Year Follow-up." *Journal of Literacy Research* 28.1 (1996): 173-195.

Piaget, J. *Play, Dreams, and Imitation*. New York: Free Press, 1962.

Pine, J., and E. Lieven. "Re-analyzing Rote Learned Phrases: Individual Differences and the Transition to Multi-Word Speech." *Journal of Child Language* 20 (1993): 551-571.

Pollock, J.S. *Reading Recovery Program 1991-92. Elementary and Secondary Education Act. Final Evaluation Report*. Columbus Public Schools, OH. Dept. of Program Evaluation, 1992.

Pouthas, V. "Temporal Regulation of Behaviour in Humans: A Developmental Approach." *Behaviour Analysis in Theory and Practice: Contributions and Controversies*. Ed. D. E. Blackman and H. Lejeune. Hove: Lawrence Earlbaum Associations, 1990. 33-52.

Powell, D. and D. Hornsby. *Learning Phonics and Spelling in a Whole Language Classroom*. New York: Scholastic, 1993.

Pugh, A., and L. Pugh. *Music In The Early Years: Teaching And Learning In The First Three Years Of School*. New York: Routledge, 1998.

Rakic, P. "Corticogenesis in Human and Non-Human Primates." *The Cognitive Neurosciences* (1997): 127-145. Ed. M. Gazzaniga. Cambridge, MA: MIT Press.

Rakison, D.H., and G.E. Butterworth. "Infants' Attention to Object Structure in Early Categorization." *Developmental Psychology* 34 (1998): 1310-1325.

Raphael, T.E., and K.H. Au. *Literature-Based Instruction: Re-shaping the Curriculum*. Norwood, MA: Christopher-Gordon Publishers, Inc., 1998.

Reid, E.R. *Enriching a Child's Literacy Environment (ECLE)*. Salt Lake City, UT: Exemplary Center for Reading Instruction, Reid Foundation, 1993.

Repacholi, B.M., and A. Gopnik. "Early Reasoning About Desires: Evidence from 14- and 18-Month-Olds." *Developmental Psychology* 33 (1997): 12-21.

Rescorla, L. and E. Schwartz. "Outcomes of Toddlers With Specific Expressive Language Delay." *Applied Psycholinguistics* 11 (1990): 393-408.

Rich, S. "Restoring Power to Teachers: The Impact of Whole Language." *Language Arts* 7 (1985): 717-721.

Robinson, F., E. Sulzby. *Parents, Children, and "Favorite" Books: An Interview Study*. University of Illinois Press, 1983.

Robinson, V.B. *The Performance of Early Readers and Pre-Readers on Concrete Operational Tasks*. M.Ed. Thesis, Pennsylvania State University, 1987.

Roe, M., and C. Vukelich. "Portfolio Implementation: What About R for Realistic?" *Journal of Research in Childhood Education* 9.1 (1994): 5-14.

Ross, E.P. *Pathways to Thinking: Strategies for Developing Independent Learners K-8*. Norwood, MA: Christopher-Gordon Publishers, Inc., 1998.

Routman, R. *Transitions*. Portsmouth, NH: Heinemann, 1988.

Rubin, D. *Diagnosis and Correction in Reading Instruction*. Third Edition. Des Moines, IA: Allyn and Bacon, 1997.

Rutter, M. "Clinical Implications of Attachment Concepts: Retrospect and Prospect." *Journal of Child Psychology and Psychiatry and Allied Disciplines* 36 (1995): 549-571.

Sanacore, J. *Encouraging All Children, Including At-Risk Learners, To Make Choices about Their Literacy Learning*. Project Description for Course of Action by University of Oregon, 1998.

Schickedanz, J.A., M.L. Pergantis, J. Kanosky, A. Blaney, and J. Ottinger. *Curriculum in Early Childhood: A Resource Guide for Preschool and Kindergarten Teachers*. Needham Heights, MA: Allyn and Bacon, 1987.

Senechal, M., J. LeFevre, Hudson, and E.P. Lawson. "Knowledge of Storybooks as a Predictor of Young Children's Vocabulary." *Journal of Educational Psychology* 87 (1996): 218-229.

Shore, C., W.E. Dixon, and P.J. Bauer. "Measures of Linguistic and Non-Linguistic Knowledge of Objects in the Second Year." *First Language* 15 (1995): 189-202.

Siegler, Robert. *Emerging Minds: The Process of Change in Children's Thinking*. New York: Oxford University Press, Inc., 1998.

Silberg, J. *Games to Play With Babies*. Beltsville, MD: Gryphon House, 1993.

Silberg, J. *Games to Play With Toddlers*. Beltsville, MD: Gryphon House, 1993.

Singer, D.G., and J.L. Singer. *The House of Make-Believe: Children's Play and the Developing Imagination*. Cambridge, Mass.: Harvard University Press, 1990.

Sirevaag, A.M., and W.T. Greenough. "Plasticity of GFAP-Immunoreactive Astrocyte Size and Number in Visual Cortex of Rats Reared in Complex Environments." *Brain Research* 540 (1991): 273-278.

Sirevaag, A.M., J.E. Black, and W.T. Greenough. "Astrocyte Hypertrophy in the Dentate Gyrus of Young Male Rats Reflects Variation of Individual Stress Rather Than Group Environmental Complexity Manipulations." *Experimental Neurology* 111 (1991): 74-79.

Slade, A. "Symbolic Play and Separation Individuation: A Naturalistic Study." *Bulletin of the Menninger Clinic* 50 (1986): 541-563.

Smith, F. "Learning to Read: The Never-Ending Debate." *Phi Delta Kappan* 73.6 (1992): 432-441.

Smith, P.K. "Does Play Matter? Functional and Evolutionary Aspects of Animal and Human Play." *Behavioral and Brain Sciences* 5 (1982): 139-184.

Smith, P.K. "Rough-and-Tumble Play, Aggression, and Dominance: Perception and Behavior in Children's Encounters." *Human Development* 33 (1990): 271-282.

Snyder, J. *Assessment of Children's Reading: A Comparison of Sources of Evidence*. National Center for Restructuring Education, Schools and Teaching. New York: Columbia Univ., Teachers Coll., 1993.

Sroute, A. "Socioemotional Development." *Handbook of Infant Development*. Ed. J. Osofsky. New York: Wiley, 1979.

Stahl, S., J. Osborn, and F. Lehr. *Beginning to Read: Thinking and Learning About Print - A Summary*. Champaign, IL: University of Illinois, Center for the Study of Reading, 1989.

Stahl, S.A. "Fluency-Oriented Reading Instruction." *Reading Research Report No.79*. Athens, GA: National Reading Research Center, 1997.

Stahl, S.A. *Beginning To Read: Thinking and Learning About Print*. Ed. Marilyn Jager Adams. Cambridge: Bolt, Beranek and Newman, Inc., 1990.

Stark, R.E. "Stages of Speech Development in the First Year of Life." *Child Phonology: Production* Vol. 1. Ed. G.H. Yeni-Komshian, J.F. Kavanagh, and C.A. Ferguson. New York: Academic Press, 1980. 93-112.

Stern, D.N. *The Interpersonal World of the Infant*. New York: Basic Books, 1985.

Sternberg, R. *Thinking Styles: Keys to Understanding Student Performance*. Phi Delta Kappan 1990. 366-371.

Stevens, R.J. *A Cooperative Learning Approach to Elementary Reading and Writing Instruction: Long-Term Effects*. Report No. 42. Baltimore, MD: Center for Research on Elementary and Middle Schools, 1989.

Stipex, D. "Children's Perceptions of Their Own and Their Classmates' Ability." *Journal of Educational Psychology* 73 (1981): 404-410.

Strickland, D.S., and L.M. Morrow. *Emerging Literacy: Young Children Learn To Read and Write*. Newark, DE: International Reading Association, 1994.

Stromswold, K. "The Cognitive and Neural Bases of Language Acquisition." *The Cognitive Neurosciences*. Ed. M. Gazzaniga. Cambridge, MA: MIT Press, 1997. 127-145.

Sulzby, E. "Assessment of Emergent Literacy: Storybook Reading (Assessment)." *Reading Teacher* 44.7 (1991): 498-500.

Sulzby, E. "Children's Emergent Reading of Favorite Storybooks: A Developmental Study." *Reading Research Quarterly* 20.4 (1985): 458-81.

Sulzby, E. *Children's Storybook Reading: Longitudinal Study of Parent-Child Interaction and Children's Independent Functioning*. Chicago: Spencer Foundation, 1987.

Swanson, H.L. "Influence of Metacognitive Knowledge and Aptitude on Problem-Solving." *Journal of Educational Psychology* 82.2 (1990): 306-314.

Thal, D., and E. Bates. "Language and Gesture in Late Talkers." *Journal of Speech and Hearing Research* 31 (1988): 115-123.

Thal, D., S. Tobias, and D. Morrison. "Language and Gesture in Late Talkers: A 1-Year Follow-Up." *Journal of Speech and Hearing Research* 34 (1991): 604-612.

Thal, D.J., E. Bates, J. Goodman, and J. Jahn-Samilo. "Continuity of Language Abilities: An Exploratory Study of Late- and Early-Talking Toddlers." *Developmental Neuropsychology* 13(3) (1997): 239-273.

Tomasello, M. and M. Farrar. "Joint Attention and Early Language." *Child Development* 57 (1986): 1454-1463.

Tomasello, M., G. Conti-Ramsden, and B. Ewert. "Young Children's Conversations With Their Mothers and Fathers: Differences in Breakdown and Repair." *Journal of Child Language* 17 (1990): 115-130.

Tomasello, M., R. Strosberg, and N. Akhtar. "Eighteen-Month-Old Children Learn Words in Non-Ostensive Contexts." *Journal of Child Language* 23 (1996): 157-176.

Torgesen, J.K. "Longitudinal Studies of Phonological Processing and Reading." *Journal of Learning Disabilities.* 27.5 (1994): 276-286.

Torgesen, J.K. and T.A. Baker. "Computers As Aids in the Prevention and Remediation of Reading Disabilities." *Learning Disability Quarterly* 18.2 (1995): 76-87.

Trehub, S.E. "Singing as a Parenting Tool." *Early Childhood Connections.* Spring (1999). 8-14.

Trehub, S.E. "The Perception of Musical Patterns by Human Infants: The Provision of Similar Patterns By Their Parents." *Comparative Perception: Basic Mechanisms* Vol. 1. Ed. M.A. Berkley and W.C. Stebbins. New York: Wiley, 1990. 429-459.

Trehub, S.E., A.M. Unyk, S.B. Kamenetsky, D.S. Hill, LJ. Trainor, J.L. Henderson, and M. Saraz. "Mothers' and Fathers' Singing to Infants." *Developmental Psychology* 33 (1997): 500-507.

Trehub, S.E., and LJ. Trainor. "Singing to Infants: Lullabies and Play Songs." *Advances in Infancy Research* Ed. C. Rovee-Collier, L. Lipsitt, and H. Hayne. Stamford, CT: Ablex, 1998. 43-77.

Trehub, S.E., B.A. Schneider, and M. Endman. "Developmental Changes in Infant's Sensitivity to Octave-Band Noises." *Journal of Experimental Child Psychology* 29 (1980): 283-293.

Trelease, J. *The Read-Aloud Handbook.* New York, NY: Penguin Books, 1995.

Tucker. "Returning to the Public School Classroom as a First Grade Teacher: Putting Theory into Practice." *Illinois State University College of Education NEWS* 3 (1996): 1-10.

Ullery, L. *Developing and Sustaining Early Literacy Experiences for Pre-kindergarten Children Through a Systematic Program of Home/School Involvement.* Paper presented at University of Florida. Florida: University of Florida, 1993.

Vasta, R., M.M. Haith, and S.A. Miller. *Child Psychology: The Modern Science.* 2nd ed. New York: John Wiley and Sons, 1995.

Vukelich, C. "Assessing Young Children's Literacy: Documenting Growth and Informing Practice (Early Childhood)." *Reading Teacher* 50.5 (1997): 430-434.

Vukelich, C. "Effects of Play Interventions on Young Children's Reading of Environmental Print." *Early Childhood Research Quarterly* 9.2 (1994): 153-170.

Vukelich, C. "Play: A Context for Exploring the Functions, Features, and Meaning of Writing with Peers." *Language Arts* 70.5 (1993): 386-392.

Vukelich, C., and M. Roe. "Imitations of Life: Authenticity in Classroom Literacy Events." *Contemporary Education* 66.3 (1995): 179-182.

Waring-Chaffee, M.B. " 'Ready or Not, Here I Come!': Investigations in Children's Emergence as Readers and Writers." *Young Children* 49.6 (1994): 52-55.

Waxman, S.R., and D.B. Markow. "Words as Invitations to Form Categories: Evidence From 12- to 13-month-old Infants." *Cognitive Psychology* 29 (1995): 257-302.

Weaver, C. *Jevon Doesn't Sit at the Back Anymore.* New York: Scholastic, 1990.

Weaver, C. *Reading Process and Practice* 2nd ed. Portsmouth, NH: Heinemann, 1994.

Weaver, C. *Understanding Whole Language: Front Principles to Practice.* Portsmouth, NH: Heinemann, 1990.

Weiner, B. "An Attributional Theory of Achievement, Motivation and Emotion." *Psychological Review* 92.4 (1985): 548-573.

Weir, B. "A Research Base for Pre-kindergarten Literacy Programs." *Reading Teacher* 42.7 (1989): 456-460.

Welsh, M.C. and B.F. Pennington. "Assessing Frontal Lobe Functioning in Children: Views from Developmental Psychology." *Developmental Neuropsychology* 4 (1988): 199-230.

Werker, J.F., and R.C. Tees. "Cross-Language Speech Perception: Evidence for Perceptual Re-organization During the First Year of Life." *Infant Behavior and Development* 7 (1984): 49-63.

Werker, J.F., L.B. Cohen, V.L. Lloyd, M. Casasola, and C.L. Stager. "Acquisition of Word-Object Associations by 14-Month-Old Infants." *Developmental Psychology* 34 (1998): 1289-1309.

Werker, J.F., V.L Lloyd, J.E. Pegg, and L. Polka. "Putting the Baby in the Bootstraps: Toward a More Complete Understanding of the Role of the Input in Infant Speech Processing." *Signal to Syntax: Bootstrapping from Speech to Grammar in Early Acquisition.* Ed. J.L. Morgan, K. Demuth, et al. Mahwah, NJ: Lawrence Erlbaum Associates, Inc., 1996. 427-447.

White, B.L. *Educating the Infant and Toddler.* Lexington, MA: D.C. Heath and Company, 1988.

White, B.L. *The New First Three Years of Life.* New York: Fireside, 1995.

Whitehurst, G.J., and D.A. Crone. "Social Constructivisim, Posivitism, and Facilitated Communication." *The Journal of the Association of Persons with Severe Handicaps* 19 (1990): 191-195.

Whitehurst, G.J. "The Stony Brook Emergent Literacy Curriculum." Stony Brook, NY: published by the author.

Whitehurst, G.J. "Treatment of Children with Language Disorders." *British Journal of Clinical Psychology* 33 (1990): 579-581.

Whitehurst, G.J., and J.E. Fischel. "Early Developmental Language Delay: What, If Anything, Should the Clinician Do About It?" *Journal of Child Psychology and Psychiatry* 35 (1995): 613-648.

Whitehurst, G.J., D.H. Arnold, J.N. Epstein, A.L. Angell, M. Smith, and J.E. Fischel. "A Picture Book Reading Intervention in Daycare and Home for Children from Low-Income Families." *Developmental Psychology* 30 (1993), 679-689.

Whitehurst, G.J., J.N. Epstein, A. Angell, A.C. Payne, D. Crone, and J.E. Fischel. "Outcomes of an Emergent Literacy Intervention in Head Start." *Journal of Educational Psychology* 84 (1994): 541-556.

Williams, P., and S.W. Lundsteen. *Home Literacy Portfolios: Cooperative Tools for Assessing Parents' Involvement in Their Pre-kindergarten Child's Literacy Development.* Paper Presented at University of Texas. Texas: University of Texas, 1997.

Williams, S.M., and P.A. Silva. "Some Factors Associated with Reading Ability: A Longitudinal Study." *Educational Research* 27.3 (1985): 159-168.

Wilson, M. S. *Helping Young Children Gain in Literacy: Implementing a Whole Language Approach in Pre-kindergarten.* Paper Presented at Nova University. Nova University, 1992.

Wittrock, M. C. "A Generative Model of Mathematics Learning." *Journal for Research in Mathematics Education* 5 (1974): 181-197.

Wittrock, M. C. "Generative Processes of Comprehension." *Educational Psychologist* 24 (1990): 345-376.

Wittrock, M. C. "Generative Teaching of Comprehension." *Elementary School Journal* 92 (1991): 167-182.

Wittrock, M. C. "Learning as Generative Process." *Educational Psychologist* 11 (1974): 87-95.

Wittrock, M. C. "Metacognition." *Strategic Learning: Skill, Will, and Self-Regulation* Ed. C. E. Weinstein and B. L. McCombs. Hillsdale, NJ: Erlbaum, 1995.

Wittrock, M. C. "Reading Comprehension." *Neuropsychological and Cognitive Processes of Reading.* Ed. F. J. Pirozzolo and M. C. Wittrock. New York: Academic, 1981.

Wittrock, M. C. and K. Alesandrini. "Generation of Summaries and Analogies and Analytic and Holistic Abilities." *American Educational Research Journal* 27.3 (1990): 489-502.

Woodward, A. L, E. M. Markman, and C. M. Fitzsimmons. "Rapid Word Learning in 13- and 18-Month-Olds." *Developmental Psychology* 30.4 (1994): 553-566.

Younger, Barbara A. and Leslie B. Cohen. "Developmental Change in Infants' Perception of Correlations Among Attributes." *Child Development* 57 (1986): 803-815.

Zahn-Waxler, C., M. and Radke-Yarrow. "The Origins of Empathic Concern." *Motivation and Emotion.* 14.2 (1990): 107-130.

Zahn-Waxler, C., M. Radke-Yarrow, E. Wagner, and M. Chapman. "Development of Concern for Others." *Developmental Psychology* 28 (1992): 126-136.

Zimmerman, B. J. and M. Martinez-Pons. "Student Differences in Self-Regulated Learning: Relating Grade, Sex, and Giftedness to Self-Efficacy and Strategy Use." *Journal of Educational Psychology* 82 (1990): 51-59.

Index